The Stepcare Recovery Guide

A STEP BY STEP EXPERIENTIAL LEARNING APPROACH TO OVERCOMING THE LIFE-SHATTERING EFFECTS OF SUBSTANCE ABUSE

by

Gary W. Reece, Ph.D.

Wipf and Stock Publishers
150 West Broadway • Eugene OR 97401

AUTHOR'S NOTE

This publication is designed to provide accurate and authoritative information in regard to the subject matter covered. It is sold with the understanding that through its preparation and publication, the author is not engaged in rendering psychological, financial, legal, medical or other professional services. If expert assistance or counseling is needed, the services of a competent professional should be sought.

Wipf and Stock Publishers
199 W 8th Ave, Suite 3
Eugene, OR 97401

Stepcare Recovery Guide
By Reece, Gary W.
Copyright © 2001 by Reece, Gary W. All rights reserved.
Softcover ISBN-13: 978-1-57910-673-7
Hardcover ISBN-13: 978-1-4982-4692-7
eBook ISBN-13: 978-1-7252-4119-0
Publication date 7/24/2001

DEDICATION

This guide is written as I stand in the circle of friends, family and colleagues whose loving support has made the journey possible, whatever wisdom and strength I have gained in my own quest I offer to the reader who may come upon this artifact and gain something; a new perspective, or sustanence perhaps. That is all any of us can offer another, our compassion, wisdom, strength, hope and legacy of our struggle.

I would like to specifically acknowledge my son Brandon Scott Reece who has devoted much time and effort in supporting my efforts as a writer. He has designed the cover and also actively manages the Stepcare web site. It is a joy to have his support and friendship, it is truly a relationship which transcends father and son.

Gary W. Reece, Ph.D.
Sierra Madre, California
2001

STEPCARE

TABLE OF CONTENTS

STEPCARE

INTRODUCTION

Substance abuse is one of the major public health issues confronting our country today and is a worldwide problem of major dimension. In the United States 18% of the population experience a substance abuse disorder at some point in their lives.

MARC GALANTER M.D.

The life of an addict who, by definition, is chemically dependent on a mind altering substance, is characterized by two things: disintegration and bondage. Psychological, physical, economic, social, career, and family problems abound; this is the downward cycle of disintegration. Secondly, the life of addiction is one of bondage because the addict has formed a coercive bond with a substance. The addict comes to experience life as slavery, typified by torturous periods of lack of control. Like Humpty Dumpty, all the King's horses and all the King's men cannot put him back together again. Unlike Humpty Dumpty, however, the addict need not be a passive victim who is destined to being perpetually shattered. The key in the equation is the addict. If you are motivated, willing to participate in your own recovery, given adequate resources and a caring and supportive recovery environment, you can recover. You can regain your lost power. This, in brief, is the basic philosophy of *STEPCARE*: the proper tools, and a caring and supportive recovery environment whose goal is empowerment.

The strategy for recovery in this program is based on the belief that addiction is a complex disorder that has its roots in the physical, emotional, psychological, social, and family history of each unique individual. Although addicts share a common affliction, each is unique in response to the problem. I am convinced that a model founded on a multi—disciplinary approach is, therefore, required; one that considers the complexities of the physical, cultural, psychological and family factors that contribute to the overwhelming need for psycho—active chemicals. When addicts, and their families are involved in a systematic, active, supportive, educational and skills development program, there is a very good chance for success.

The goal is recovery. Recovery in my model is not just sobriety, although that is the first requirement. Recovery means becoming aware of the process and the problems that led to reliance on chemicals. Recovery also means learning new habits and coping skills that lead to more effective living. This, in turn, will lead to enhanced feelings of competence and self—esteem. Recovery means starting now! You cannot be any place other than where you are now; as much as you wish the problem didn't exist, or would like it to go away. You are where you are, now! The problem must be confronted now! Denial, that deadly defense, must be penetrated and discarded. Honesty with yourself and others will restore the lost respect and self—esteem that are the first casualties of addiction. Recovery is up to you. This perilous moment may be your greatest opportunity to begin a new life; a different life.

Recovery, that tortuous journey back from the living dead, may begin with a moment of clarity that could take many forms. For some, it may be a brilliant awakening that penetrated your consciousness as you were sitting in the drunk tank with other illustrious citizens of noble pursuits. You realized, perhaps, that something was amiss. For others, it comes gradually as you pass through the stages of addiction which lead to losing your job, health, family, and other prized mementos. In whatever form the enlightenment came, it is usually accompanied by a great deal of pain. The pain of addiction must be sufficient to break through denial.The pain is a messenger; it is your best friend. It is trying to tell you that you are in trouble and that your life is not working as you are currently leading it.

Finally, the messenger is trying to tell you that if you do not make some drastic changes, probably, you will die. Addiction leads, inevitably, to self—destruction.

If enlightenment has not come yet, and you find yourself in a program because of coercion from a boss, the police, or a family member "who just doesn't understand you," then I hope that somewhere you will get it.

Get what? The basic idea that you have gone down a very commonly traveled path that leads to ruin. Although there is a great deal of loneliness, paradoxically, you have a lot of company.

The purpose of this first section is to introduce you to some basic ideas and help you assess where you are right now.

In other words, develop a perspective that will help you understand the path that led to your particular predicament. This kind of understanding is not a cure all. But we do try to build a fundamental base of self—understanding. Beyond this base of self—understanding, we will try to add some new tools for coping with specific life problems. The basic idea here is that addiction is an acquired problem that began as a solution to a life problem. I believe that you have, for very personal reasons, developed a physical and a psychological dependence on chemicals.

Psychological dependence has occurred because the chemicals you have been using are psycho—active. That is to say, they change consciousness and alter your mood in one way or another. Over time, the chemically dependent person relies increasingly on a change in feeling or consciousness to cope more effectively with self, reality, or others. Most people gain some pleasure or immediate benefit from consuming chemicals. This is the reason for using them. I believe addicts have learned to self—medicate. If the results were immediately painful or did nothing, there would be no reason for their use. Chemicals are powerfully reinforcing because they have an immediate effect that may be both physically and psychologically pleasurable, as well as socially encouraged and supported.

Becoming chemically dependent is a seductive, tricky, business and it affects everyone differently. Each person is at risk in seemingly hundreds of various ways. I want to help you understand the process of becoming chemically dependent.

4

Physiological addiction is acquired through different channels than psychological dependence. The mechanism is very complex and we do not need to go into all of the technical reasons now. In simple terms, the body, because it is wonderfully adept at meeting the demands of adaptation, begins to set in motion the necessary chemical changes to handle the chemicals ingested. As we put in more chemicals, the body works harder to adapt to the new level of intake. Gradually, over time, the body requires more chemical to get the original benefit of whatever is used. When this is coupled with the increased psychological dependence, a very powerful compulsion to use is set in motion.

This recovery program is designed to help you understand the process of becoming chemically dependent. To do so, you must understand your personal history, your present life stressors and contributing risk factors.

People who have the highest risk of becoming addicted have been raised in a family where one or more parents were alcoholic or otherwise addicted. Secondly, a high risk person is someone who has poor coping skills, is under a lot of stress, and has found a connection to the secret of better living through chemistry. In short, it is a combination of vulnerability caused by inherited biological predispositions, psychological susceptibility caused by family history, and current vulnerability caused by multiple stressors. In my experience, those whose lifestyles have become adapted to chemicals have done so to escape from an unhappy existence. They have found that the rewards of living in an altered state of consciousness outweigh all the costs of the destructive—chemically dependent lifestyle. For these people, a chemically free life feels like no life at all. Therefore, a new lifestyle is critical to any recovery program; sobriety is not enough.

In sum, addiction is a complex problem requiring intervention at various levels. Addicts have been found to have a shared cluster of problems. These problems include poor coping skills, low self—esteem, difficulties in interpersonal relationships, difficulty in communication, problems in recognizing, experiencing and expressing feelings, inability to experience intimacy in love relationships, and dysfunctional family lives. *STEPCARE* is a program that targets each of these problem areas and then actively promotes the development of competency through a process of learning, rehearsal, support and positive feedback. *STEPCARE* is comprehensive, multi—disciplinary, and bridges the gap between the mental health community and the twelve step recovery community.

STEPCARE is based on learning to cope, finding pleasure, feeling competent, building self—esteem, learning to handle shame, guilt, anxiety, and depression, having friends and relaxing without chemicals. I want to help you reverse the downward cycle of failure and begin to build patterns of success and hope. Some find it hard to even imagine that all of this is possible. I intend to help you, one step at a time, to regain the power you have given up.I will teach you how to care for yourself and build bridges to other caring people.

Finally, reading this manual is only one step in recovery. It has been my experience that successful recovery needs several elements. The first is a quality recovery environment. This is why I recommend A.A. or some related group support program where the addict can gain support, positive feedback, acceptance and encouragement. A second element is some form of counseling to gain awareness and work on underlying problems that may be of a chronic nature.

Thirdly, this manual is designed to be a supplement to A.A. and therapy; it is not a substitute. It is intended as a systematic approach to recovery that gives practical steps to help in integrating the emotional, behavioral and cognitive elements of the journey.

In essence, addiction creates a multitude of problems. Recovery requires intelligent, caring, consistent work to repair the damage, cope with the immediate symptoms of withdrawal and rebuild a livable, sustainable life without chemicals. If this is not done, the result is often the half—lived life of dysfunctional sobriety, quiet desperation and frequent relapse, or even worse, the continued bondage and disintegration of addiction. The next step is up to you!

NOTES

RECOVERY

The first principle of recovery is empowerment.
Judith Lewis Herman M.D.

Recovery is an ambiguous word. It means many things to many people. It is also very personal in that a person who is recovering views the process much differently than one who is not. In this chapter we will try to give the term more precision as we seek to understand its basic elements. What is involved under this umbrella term? To answer this question we need to know from what we are recovering. Is it cancer or a sprained ankle? The problem and solution define each other. In the case of addiction we have seen an evolution from defining it as a "moral problem" where a "sinner" needs salvation to a disease that requires a different approach. If it is a disease, how is it transmitted and what is its cure? Is it learned, some form of mental Illness, or is it some combination of not clearly understood processes? Many of these questions are being debated in the field of addiction today. These academic questions, though important, have an ivory tower quality to them. In the laboratory, where the brain sizes of alcoholic rats are compared to "normals," researchers are trying to isolate and perhaps locate the gene that may be responsible for addiction proneness. The temptation is to look for a single bullet or build our position on a single cause. Most of the research is leaning toward a model which is based on multiple causality.

The reality of addiction, however, is never abstract. It always involves suffering, and not just that of the addict, but all of those whose lives are touched by him or her. The bottom line about addiction is suffering. The addict has a very personal war with an overwhelming and devouring enemy. This struggle is against and with compulsive, self—destructive forces. Recovery is about, in its best sense, regaining power, control, meaning and self—respect. And finally, recovery is about life and death.

Let us look at the recovery process to understand its basic elements and by doing so make it more of a realistic possibility. I am reminded of a story told by Milton Erickson, a famous psychiatrist. He was describing recovery as a process of using control. He said that Custer would not have been massacred if he could have gotten the Indians to come over the hill one at a time. I think this is the importance of the idea of one day at a time. Recovery is about learning to break things down into their most basic elements and then starting to rebuild from there. After all, it's one thing to read about the structure and history of life boats in the comfort of your living room; it is, however, an entirely different matter when viewed from the deck of the Titanic. It is important to never miss sight of the fact that recovery is always a lonely and very personal struggle.

This volume is based on a social learning model, in which I am seeking to build a bridge between the recovery community of alcoholics and narcotics anonymous and the psychological community. The two have historically often been at odds. I believe much of this has been due to looking at different aspects of the same problem. My goal is to create a framework for understanding the very foundations of recovery and to build a practical handbook from this base. I believe that no one is well served by the differences in philosophy and methodology that have divided the two communities.

In my own experience, I have found that individuals I have worked with who have substance abuse problems have had a better chance of recovery when the best of both worlds has been used. I have seen people recovering who have just been involved with A.A.. I have seen people recover who did it on their own. But these people have a common problem. Though they have become sober, they still have considerable problems in living. This has led me to conclude that sobriety is not enough. Yes, of course, sobriety is the first condition for recovery. But recovery, in my definition, also means rebuilding shattered lives, clearing up the wreckage of the past, and learning to live with a sense of power and purpose.

My goal is to provide insight, guidance, and assistance in a practical guidebook for people who perhaps would not ordinarily seek psychological help. My approach is based on 20 years of working with sick and dying alcoholics and other addicts. I have also worked with the refugees of the battle: their devastated families. At the personal level, I can attest to the unhappiness caused by the effects of an alcoholic father on a family, and struggling with my own various addictions.

While there is, in my view, no true addictive personality, there is a commonality of problems. Addicts come from all levels of education, socioeconomic classes, and ethnic groups, but, have the common bond of their problem. This commonality of problems is the reason for the approach I have adopted in this manual. I have said that addiction is a problem with multiple causes (biological, psychological, and social.) This multiple causality is perhaps made worse or triggered by life stress. When the addiction prone person becomes physically addicted and psychologically dependent, there are powerful social learning factors that sustain the problem. Addiction is a high cost behavior. That is, the consequences lead to damage in many different areas. The most obvious ones are health and loss of job. The higher costs, though, are to self—esteem and damage to those we love.

Addiction eventually leads to the natural consequence of shame and self—contempt. Not only does the addict come to feel that way about himself, but of course, others feel the same way as well. Besides the problems of self—esteem, there is a whole constellation of related problems: poor communication, difficulty in interpersonal relationships, difficulty in dealing with feelings and poor coping skills under stress. Because addicts have similarities in problems, I believe that the most effective recovery program is one that teaches skills for living.

My fundamental conviction is that by increasing feelings of competency and interpersonal effectiveness this will lead to gains in self—esteem and more successful relationships. If we feel better about ourselves, and others, then the need to use mind altering chemicals will decrease correspondingly.

The goal is to build a practical skill base through learning and practice. This approach is based on the three A's of recovery. **Awareness, Assessment, and Action.** Recovery begins when denial ends. Therefore, the first step is **Awareness.** We must begin to live consciously and make good, responsible choices based on self—awareness. Awareness of feelings, awareness of needs, awareness of problems, awareness of wounds. Without awareness, we truly are flying blind. This is why there are so many practical exercises in this workbook. They are specifically designed to increase awareness. **Awareness** is the antidote for denial. Denial, of course, is the first line of defense against facing problems. A person who is stuck in a cycle of destructive repetition, or compulsive re—enactment of destructive behavioral patterns, is practicing denial. This deludes a person into living a lie. While we convince ourselves nothing is wrong, others around us who care are frightened by our behavior. It's like burning our house down around us while telling ourselves that a little fire is good.

Awareness opens us to feedback that is vital to our survival. Being willing to live with awareness is one thing, however, it requires active diligence, a rigorous watchfulness for the signs of trouble that will enable us to take

13

appropriate, adaptive, action. Since most of us grew up in families where awareness was not encouraged, it will require considerable practice to learn to live in awareness. The reason for this is that denial has served important defensive purposes in the past. However, it now is counterproductive.

How do we know we are on the right track? One cannot do anything about solving a problem until one first recognizes that there is a problem. This is the first step. Whether it comes by way of a brilliant flash of light, or when one hits bottom and feels the darkness of despair, it must come in some form of recognition. My life is not working: I am powerless!

Trying to gain awareness will be encountered by resistance. This will be particularly true if we were shamed, ridiculed, demeaned or punished for wanting, needing, or feeling. The more dysfunctional the family of origin, the more likely it is that we will have difficulty becoming aware of feelings. Because it was so painful to be needy, helpless, and dependent as children, we developed defenses. These defenses block awareness and create blind spots. These eventuate in living unconsciously. That is, we are out of touch with deeper emotions and conflicts that motivate us. The more unconsciously we live, the more likely we are to be living dysfunctional lives. Living with awareness leads to the possibility of a well-lived life.

Awareness informs; it allows us to be in touch with feelings that are the messenger indicating the state of our well—being at the moment. Blocking the message leads to faulty perception, anxiety, depression and low self—esteem.

It also prohibits us from feeling our feelings which leads to a deadness of spirit. This is one of the chief aims of using chemicals; to block out the pain, to anesthetize our senses.

Awareness, then, allows us to feel our feelings, it gives us more information about what is going on around us, it corrects cognitive errors that lead to a devalued sense of self and corrects the myopia that distorts perceptions. It also will help us see and expose the sacred family myths and lies that were systematically taught us. Awareness is essential for intelligent change. But it is not the only ingredient.

Historically, psychology was committed to the concept of Insight as the main ingredient in change. Subsequent experience has taught us that seeing is but the beginning of change. Yes, it is very important to be aware of our behavior and what may have caused it, but more is required if we are to change life—long destructive habits. For it is out of growing awareness that we can create a strategy for recovery and know what it is exactly we need to do to change. Seeing the problem will lead to uncovering the solution.

Awareness of what we are experiencing is critical to recovery of self—esteem. Most basically, however, self—esteem cannot be restored until we stop the dishonesty. Self—delusion leads to self—contempt. Honest appraisal restores relationships. If our relationships have been founded on deception, we may experience some difficulties when we try to get them on an honest footing. In fact, you may discover that some people prefer the lie. It is easier to engage in self—deception, to pretend that things aren't so bad. "Our marriage is wonderful; please don't tell me how you really feel about me, let's pretend everything is beautiful!" This takes two people in collusion to maintain a lie. I've had many people become angry because they come to see me for marital therapy and things got difficult when honest feelings were surfacing. "Our relationship has gotten worse since we started telling each other how we feel, can't we go back to the way it was?" Or, in the case of the parents who brought their teenager to see me and he told me about how violent and abusive his parents were when they drank. So I called mom and dad in for a conference and they took their child out of therapy because I started focusing on their relationship.

In the beginning stages it is important to practice the awareness exercises that you will learn throughout this manual. It is important to spend time each day practicing getting in touch with feelings. This is why awareness is so critical to recovery. We need to learn what our feelings are trying to tell us. And instead of chemically managing anger, learn to recognize and express it directly. The only way one can do this is to pay attention to what you are feeling; feel the feelings as deeply as possible and then understand their meaning for you. You may have to try a number of exercises to find out what helps to crack the code. Once we have begun the process of gaining awareness, it follows naturally that we must learn to process the information. What do we do with all this awareness? Isn't ignorance bliss? Again, because of our histories, we may have some real ambivalence about this awareness business. This leads to the second stage in recovery: **Assessment.**

This step is important because it involves learning to develop rational, cognitive skills that lead to less impulsive behavior. I believe the phrase "stinkin thinkin" is used a lot in A.A. circles. Much of dysfunctional behavior comes from dysfunctional thinking which leads naturally to irrational thoughts and destructive-faulty decisions. The entire premise of a cognitive behavioral approach to psychotherapy stems from this idea. If we can change our thoughts, we can change behavior. We will learn how to do this in the following sections. It is a truism that feeling without thought is chaos. Learning to assess our feelings and behavior is critical to recovery. By learning to decipher the messages of feelings we can then know what it is we need to do. Ask yourself, what is the meaning of the tight muscles in the shoulders? What is the meaning of the knot in the stomach? Why am I so irritable? Every time I talk to my boss, I get a spasm in my colon, why is that? Why is my head hurting now? My children irritate me, I get enraged, why do I over-react? These are the questions we can ask ourselves if we get in the practice of interrogating our feelings on a regular basis. What am I feeling? What are the feelings trying to tell me? By learning to decode the message of our feelings, we can know ourselves better. Personally, I find the technique of writing down my feelings very helpful. Writing seems to pull things out and then puts them together so I can make sense of them. Paying attention to dreams also helps to understand what is

17

going on at a deeper level. Over the years, I have also been able to recognize my body language. A stiff neck means anger and helplessness; upset stomach—eating my anger; insomnia; fear, anger and helplessness, I'm agitated; diarrhea; I am feeling "shitty" and out of control—scared and dependent. These are just some things I have learned about my own reactions. You will notice that there are characteristic reactions you have to certain situations, also. This will restore a connection that often was lost in childhood. How can we possibly know how to meet our needs if we don't even know what we are feeling? How can we possibly be intimate with someone if we can't tell them what we are feeling and why? As one of my clients put it: "I have spent my whole life meeting every one else's needs, so when I focused on my own, I didn't have a clue. Somewhere I got lost in the shuffle." That awareness opened the door to a whole new world for my client: the inner world of her own needs, feelings, and secret desires she had been denying, to please others. Feeling our feelings leads to a greater sense of aliveness. This is a sign of recovery.

Feelings are always experienced personally. Our inner world of feelings is totally unique to us. So is the way we express our feelings. That is why we must learn what is our unique and characteristic way of expressing our feelings. I have a client who, when angry with her mother, goes on eating binges. This unique response is tied into the family pathology. Her mother is overbearing and critical; she is also manipulative and explosive. Hence, anger was not tolerated in her children. She gave them food whenever they were upset to quiet them. Now my client is trying to break the food addiction cycle by finding other ways to deal with her anger. When a person gets in touch with his/her feelings, what is seen often is not liked. For example, a woman, after extensive therapy, is struggling to face an incest issue. Her anger toward her father surfaces along with some repressed images and she feels shame and guilt for being so angry with him for what happened. Initially, she doubts herself, doubts that it happened, blames herself, but finally faces it. She has reached an important milestone in her recovery.

When we commit to honestly looking at ourselves, we are seeking to find the truth of our lives and live it. Again, this means facing ourselves and making a realistic assessment of who we are and who we have become. Usually, this also involves taking a look at the past, where it all began; facing mom, dad, the family and who they all were. To grow through the pain, we must face it honestly and then make sense of it. Because of our histories the information we are gaining might not fit with our cherished beliefs we have about ourselves and others. This comes from exposing family secrets, lies, and myths. It may also mean facing what we have done to ourselves and others. Doing this requires taking an "inventory." This can be, and usually is, a painful process.

This word **Pain** keeps coming up, often. Yes, pain is a big part of recovery; it is very painful facing up to the things about which we may feel terrible. Facing the pain we have caused others is no easy matter, either. Though this is a difficult process, it does lead to healing; it is the basis for restoration of the self and reconciliation with those whom we have harmed.

Awareness and assessment go hand in hand. We must face what we feel, feel it deeply, and face it honestly. These are the cornerstones of recovery, particularly this next step which is often a stumbling block. It is a very important aspect of assessment. **Acceptance** is a tremendous hurdle, but is an important sign of recovery, because it reveals a new attitude. It involves coming to grips with what has happened, and what has become one's life as a result. As we look at ourselves we think a common refrain, "How can I possibly accept all of this? I hate my life." Progressing from self—hatred to **Acceptance** is a struggle under the best of circumstances. What does it mean to accept? How does one gain it? Is it really possible? If you don't like it, how can you accept it? These are the questions asked me continually. We will explore these in a section to follow. Suffice it to say at this point that once we achieve acceptance, we stop being resentful.

In addition to growing more comfortable with our feelings and therefore ourselves, the understanding we acquire by deciphering the feelings becomes the royal road to self—awareness. Unraveling the mysteries of our feelings leads us on a historical quest. As we feel the pain and search for clues for the meaning of our behavior, we are led to the origin of self—the family. This, of course, is where the hard work must take place.

I have found over and over again that when I truly understand someone, their behavior makes sense. Working through these issues leads to understanding and then acceptance. No matter how bizarre it may seem, it has a kind of logic to it. But, the key is to see the problem through the other person's eyes. This is where understanding is raised to another level. It takes a particular kind of understanding to really have the ability to see from outside ourselves: this is *empathy.* When we can put ourselves in the place of others, we can truly understand what it must have been like for them. I found it much easier to deal with my parents when I could understand how they grew up and why they were the way they were. It also helped to understand what they were going through in their lives at the time I was being raised.

Understanding them freed me from the feelings of helplessness and victimization. Perhaps I could stop blaming them when I saw them as victims, too. I found that as my empathy grew, my compassion for us all increased. Yes, I can still feel angry and hurt over some of the things that happened. Yes, I regret the poverty, the lack of emotional support, the shaming and ridicule, and the extreme religiosity. But that was the way it was. That's my history. We have no control over the who, where, and what of history. These are the givens of our situation. I accept what I cannot change. In my acceptance, I changed my perspective. I re—appraised my life. This is the essence of accurate assessment. This changed perspective leads to different feelings and finally to letting go. This is another sign of recovery. As we become desensitized to the pain through repeatedly feeling and talking about it, we become less affected by it. In this process we are getting unstuck emotionally and are able to progress developmentally. This enables us to let go of what we never got; and of still wanting it.

No longer clinging to the pain of deprivation, and the sense of not having been loved enough, dramatically changes our perception of our current situations. If we enter every relationship from a position of painful deprivation we will continue to feel deprived and hence resentful, no matter how much we are loved and nurtured. Acceptance stops this, and enables us to say "I got what I got, they gave what they had to give." Life is incomplete and seldom ideal. So, if that was the way it was, now what? If we can answer with acceptance then we are free to move on to the next phase: forgiveness. We cannot move on until we forgive. Acceptance and forgiveness are the transition phases of recovery. They are the building blocks of the new life. Appropriately enough this final stage of recovery is characterized by **Action**, it is a time of rebuilding.

Awareness and **Assessment** are dead in the water if there is no action. The problem with many approaches to psychotherapy is that they do not lead to meaningful behavioral change. This can only come about through **Action**. **Action**, of course, is meaningless without **awareness** and **assessment**. It would be like going on a trip without a destination in mind. It is readily apparent that the three A's of recovery are interdependent. One doesn't work without the other. Action means not only doing things, but it also implies a different stance toward things. It also means to be active in working on not only changing behavior but also changing our perspective on life and our mental attitude. This is why I look at forgiveness as action. It is a very active process.

Forgiveness is, in the theological sense, a wiping of the slate clean, our sins are remembered no more: "though they be as crimson, they are as white as snow." This is a dramatic transformation of how we feel, think, and are perceived and perceive ourselves. The suffocating and crippling burden of guilt and shame are no more. Ah, but to forgive is Divine, at the human level it is more difficult.

To forgive is to *reframe* the entire experience. We will devote an entire chapter on learning to reframe. This is where working through, understanding, and acceptance are so crucial. These processes allow us to move to the pinnacle of forgiveness. This makes it possible to stop hating, blaming, judging, criticizing, and condemning. An attitude of self—hatred is replaced by self—love. Anger toward others is transformed into tolerance and compassion.

This transformation of our consciousness is manifested in our way of being in the world. Our behavior toward others is significantly changed; we are less resentful, less infantile in our expectations and reactions. We are more open, accepting and trusting. And of course, the most dramatic transformation is in our self—esteem. We have moved from the position of victim to victor. The transformation process has moved us from the position of the injured, helpless, needy, shamed, and self—destructive child, to one of a powerful, confident, independent guilt free, loving adult, who takes responsibility for his/her own life. This is the essence of empowered recovery. This journey has freed us from the past. But we must still learn to live now. This is where the action takes place. Because recovery is more than giving up addiction, it is more than being free from old resentments. It is as if we have cleaned house and remodeled it. Now, we get to live in it. How shall we furnish the new environment? We must act, but how shall we rebuild?

For those who have been conditioned to live with shame, abuse, rejection, isolation, and emotional impoverishment, it is inconceivable to live any other way. It is what one comes to accept as reality; a reality in which there are no other possibilities. As one client phrased it, "if my parents didn't love me, how could anyone else love me?' She continued, "They must have known what a terrible person I am, they knew my secret shame; that's why I wasn't loved." It is probably the most difficult thing in the world to overcome this problem. To learn to love when loving has been so painful or absent.

This is the ultimate task of recovery; learning to love ourselves, as well as others. In order to do this, we must change the basic perceptions about ourselves. To begin this process we have acquired new awareness about the formation of our identity and the way we maintain it through our continuous self—dialogue. To affirm ourselves means to have a positive, compassionate and caring attitude, a loving relationship with oneself. This will be manifested in self—talk that is realistic, non—judgmental, and supportive. It is most apparent when we do something we get upset with ourselves about, or attempt something that is difficult or when we fail to accomplish something important. Is the attitude angry, critical and shaming, or is it caring, accepting, and affirming? Basically, self—affirmation is feeling comfortable being the person you are. It certainly doesn't mean being perfect. It means knowing all about the problems, short comings, screw ups, faults, problems that have resulted in the "wreckage of the past" and perhaps even the present, and accepting it all as part of the self we are. Loving in spite of it all. It is also a commitment to living as best as one can; it is saying yes to life and trying to create the conditions necessary for a fulfilling life. A life that enhances rather than destroys self—esteem.

We have to start somewhere. And most of us have started the journey to self—love by getting sick and tired of feeling bad. The decision to do something about our condition was the first act of self—love. And as they say, the journey of a thousand miles begins with a single step. Everything you have been doing to get straight is one step further on the journey. This is what it is really all about. I call it self—affirmation: affirming oneself in spite of shame, guilt, and self—contempt. Self—affirmation is essential to self—esteem. It is a process that begins in awareness, grows stronger by acceptance, and now continues through forgiveness to fruition in self—affirmation. It means learning to value, to appreciate and to cherish yourself. If you do not love and prize yourself, you, who are the center of your universe, who will? I asked a client the other day about the last time she was really pleased with herself. She gave me a blank look and sat for several moments, lost in thought. Finally, she confessed it had been so long that she couldn't remember. This led to exploring her extreme expectations, continual self—criticism, and resultant disappointment with herself and others.

I often use humor with clients to point out issues. In this case I suggested she could either work a lot harder to become perfect or else reduce the expectations and become the terrible person she was afraid of being: of actualizing her negative self—image.

Self—affirmation means seeing ourselves through our own eyes. In order to do this we must develop our own values and meaning system. For in most cases the shoulds and shame come from those who were harsh, rigid, and punitive in their criticism of us. This was a manifestation of their inability to love and their need to control what they couldn't understand and feared. Self—affirmation leads to transformation of our self—image. Learning to love ourselves frees us from dependence on the love of others for self—esteem. This leads to being more independent.

Achieving psychological independence is an outgrowth of a high level of psychological development. When we achieve the ability to be self—reliant, we experience a greater degree of control, confidence, and competence. These are essential ingredients of self—esteem. Self—reliance means that I have come to the realization of the importance of my life; that it is a one time, very unique adventure. I am responsible for this precious gift, and must exercise care and diligence in expressing ownership of my very own life. It is really up to me to do something with whatever inner and outer resources are available. My continual goal is the well lived life; this takes wisdom and considerable awareness. Being self—responsible means that we don't blame others and don't depend on them for fulfilling our needs and taking care of our self—esteem.

Living responsibly also means learning to live with the natural consequences of our choices and behavior. It means to be responsible for our own needs, actions, and identity. Being autonomous is accepting the task of creating, designing, and building one's own identity. It is not the self—indulgence and selfishness of an adolescent or the unfeeling disregard of other's needs that is typical of a small child. These are immature expressions of independence. Autonomous, self—love is a very significant achievement and is a sure indicator that recovery is well in progress.

The implications of responsibility for self—esteem are single and clear. When we are responsible to ourselves, for ourselves, and to others, we are perceived as being trustworthy. We also have the confidence that we can trust ourselves. We have a basic sense of competence as a foundation for our self—esteem. When we are responsible we keep our commitments and obligations. This earns the respect of others. Again, the net result is a gain in esteem. Of course, if we fail to act responsibly, we lose trust and respect which diminishes self—esteem. We don't like ourselves and no one else does either. The irony of this is that failure to act responsibly leads to others being in control and taking responsibility for us. So we either act responsibly or lose our freedom. This lesson seems simple enough; so simple, that it often takes a lifetime to learn it.

Power, competence, and confidence, the by—products of acting responsibly are the core of self—esteem, that becomes fulfilled in a quest for recovery of our personal identity. So instead of having the identity of an addict, my new identity becomes one who is recovering, one who is on the way to empowerment. All of our rebuilding takes place in this framework.

Our quest for a new identity pays dividends of a solidity and consistency of self that is fulfilled in wholeness and well—being. Recovery, then, that began in a shattered, demeaned, and shamed sense of self leads to a transformation brought about through effort, courage, and commitment. The road to wholeness must go through the doorway of despair. When we pass through that portal we will travel the road traveled by all spiritual pilgrims.

Recovery is a spiritual process. It is not a religion, however. There are some people who are religious, who go to church on Christmas and Easter or even may go to church twice a week, but may not necessarily be spiritual. That is to say, the strength of their faith and commitment is defined by membership and attendance, but not by a commitment of their whole being. Paul Tillich, a very influential theologian of this century, said that faith is a matter of Ultimate Concern. Recovery is a matter of faith and it is our Ultimate Concern that defines our struggle. Recovery is struggling daily with one's whole self to be an authentic person. In the movie "Dances With Wolves," the Indian wise man commented, "There are many journeys in life, but the path which leads to the true self is the only one that matters." The Bible puts it another way, "what does it matter if one gains the whole world and loses his/her soul?" Thus, on our spiritual journey, relying on our higher power we are each seeking enlightenment and burdened by his/her own personal cross. A cross that mysteriously crucifies and redeems at one and the same time. It crucifies in the sense that our pain and suffering is a terrible burden and as such we cringe under its weight. It redeems us in that our very suffering leads to awareness and an opportunity to grow. It is the age old mystery of death and rebirth, the process of personal transformation that only occurs as we wrestle with our problems and seek meaningful solutions.

This growth process, our journey of transformation through recovery, does not take place in a vacuum. The recovering person often feels alone and isolated, bearing the cross alone in the struggle to regain dignity and integrity. Many times, because of addiction, all bridges have been burned and friends and loved ones have been alienated. Trust and respect, as well as relationships, have been destroyed. It is in this context that the road to recovery takes place and leads to a new level of development, interdependence and intimacy. The road to recovery cannot be traveled alone.

The best chance for survival is in the caring and supportive presence of a spiritual recovery community. It is imperative — an absolute necessity — to rejoin the human race; to reconnect with people and to overcome the ambivalence of intimate relationships. For it is in relationships that we become fully human. It is unfortunate, but true, that our greatest suffering probably occurs in relationships; herein is where the ambivalence occurs.

Because of the wounds, shame, and embarrassment, it is often hard to be around other people. It is for this reason that the quality of the recovery environment is crucial to recovery. The recovering person needs to feel safe and free from judgment in order to face the issues that brought them to that place of facing the problem.

It is essential that there be caring and active compassion. For many people, A.A. and/or N.A. are the places where this happens. It is important that one can identify with the community in the shared bond of a common problem. Finding this safe place can be a problem. Sometimes it takes several meetings in order to get comfortable or maybe even several different groups have to be tried before there is a connection. Many times, because of denial or shame, the addict cannot or does not want to be around people who admit they have a problem that is beyond their coping power.

Nevertheless, I have yet to see anyone recover by going it alone. The research is clear, it is the quality of the recovery environment which foundational to the recovery project. In order to get beyond sobriety to being a human being again we need a caaring context. Once the connection is made then the next step is to reveal the pain and misery in an atmosphere of acceptance. This is where the healing begins. To be loved in spite of ourselves is the highest state of grace.

Caring, trust, acceptance, forgiveness, compassion and inclusiveness are the hallmark of a recovery community. Just as these qualities are essential for the newborn baby to be offered by parents, so too, the recovering person is like a newborn. It is essential to recovery, and to healing, that the recovering person have this resource available at all times in order to be nurtured back to life. It is, in fact, a life support system that needs to be established in the first moments of recovery.

The secrets of recovery are found in reconnecting to our basic self and in regaining the ability to relate and be intimate through nurturance. In this way, the shattered self is healed and the bonds of addiction are broken. To maximize the possibility of success, I believe one who is struggling to recover must use as many resources as possible. That is why a supportive recovery environment is essential. Good friends, family, the fellowship of recovering addicts, a sponsor; all of these enhance the possibility of success. It goes without saying, recovery is not possible while continuing to use the chemical on which you are dependent. In fact, giving up whatever chemical on which you are dependent may delay other recovery stages until you are stabilized and off the substances. Getting clean and staying clean may require a highly structured program. The degree of structure depends on you and how much help you need in this area.

Finally, recovery is a journey with no fixed destination. It is the struggle to overcome, to deal authentically with one's life and to regain self—esteem. This is the heroic aspect of recovery. When viewed in this light, one can stop trying to be fixed or to have it made. As a process, recovery is an active verb, it is always something I am in the act of doing. In this regard, then, recovery is a lifestyle. Just as addiction is a way of life, so one must change the whole way of life that led to the problem. We must learn that we are the problem; the author, director, and actor in this little melodrama of our lives.

CHAPTER 1

RECOVERY

EXERCISE 1

Recovery has been described as a journey. As part of understanding your journey and yourself, it is helpful to look back at the road you have traveled that has brought you to this place. Write an autobiography. Give it a title. Divide it into chapters. Give each chapter of your life a title. Place particular emphasis upon choices, significant life changing events and crossroads. Who were the significant characters? How did they influence you? How did you get to where you are today? How do you feel about the place you are in today?

After spending time writing your story, look at it for themes and patterns. What do you see? Remember, your story is a work in progress, if we fail to learn from our mistakes we will continue to repeat them. We do not have to be prisoners of our past.

CHAPTER 1

RECOVERY

EXERCISE 2

1. Whose problem is it?

A fundamental truth in recovery is that recovery does not begin until the person owns the problem. Ownership of the problem can be looked at in several different ways.

(1) There is no problem

I have had numerous clients assume this basic position. One classic case I vividly remember was the client in my waiting room who ran into the door, stumbled into a chair, bounced off a wall, and then said he was just tired. We did a blood alcohol level that was 3 times the allowable level of .08 and he insisted the lab "screwed up" the results.

Yes _____ No _____ This is my position

Explain why you do or do not have a problem.

(2) My wife, family, employer, courts think I have a problem. and have referred me for treatment.
I do not agree because:

(A) They do not understand

(B) They are too sensitive—they have a problem with my behavior

(C) A series of bad luck has caused people to label me as having a problem

Check above any that apply to you.

34

Whose Problem Is It Anyway?

Check below any that apply to you

    (A) I can quit any time

    (B) I can control it

    (C) It's not a problem because:

        (1)   I don't do it all the time

        (2)   All my friends do it

        (3)   I'll be careful and control it

(3) When others think you have a problem, you have a problem. Describe what you can do to get out of trouble with them—in other words, be able to continue what you want to do without being hassled by them.

3.   I have a problem   _____Yes _____No

    Describe in your terms:

        1. When is it a problem?

        2. What exactly is the problem? Describe what happens — when— and how you handle it and what the consequences are.

3. Describe your life when the problem is not occurring. How are things different?

(4) I have a problem but there is nothing that can be done about it.   Yes?_____No?_____

Many times people feel so discouraged, defeated, and overwhelmed by the problem that they think there is no hope.

This is a position that I believe can be changed by:

  A.   Accepting that there is a problem.

  B.   Owning the problem.

  C.   Learning as much about the problem as possible.

  D.   Carefully designing a recovery strategy.

  E.   Wanting it more than anything.

  F.   Enlisting the help of others who are in recovery.

  G.   Enacting the recovery strategy one step at a time.

CHAPTER 1

RECOVERY

EXERCISE 3

Your Power/Helplessness Index

Very helpless all the time   _____

Sometimes helpless   _____

Helpless but only in this area   _____

Seldom Helpless   _____

Rarely, if ever, helpless   _____

RECOVERY CONTRACT

I am willing to work toward recovering from the

problem of _____
            Describe problem specifically

by doing _____
         Describe specifically recovery steps

My recovery goals are:_____

_____

_____

_____

_____

Signed: _____

Witnessed by: _____

NOTES

CHAPTER 2

STRESS AND CHEMNICAL DEPENDENCY

> An important component in the area of substance abuse is
> the availability of coping skills that can be employed to deal
> effectively with stress.
>
> G. Alan Marlatt, Ph.D.

Current research in the literature on substance abuse is
looking at a lot of different factors believed to be involved
in the complex problem of addiction. Such factors as
hereditary predisposition, learning, cultural values and the
interaction that they might have has led to fruitful insights.
Recently focus on the role of addiction in the family has
helped us understand the critical importance of early
childhood experience and family structure in the lives of
addicts.

Research continues to look at the brain chemistry of
addicts to see how it might be different from "normals". The
personality of an addict has been researched for years. The
sum of all this research has been to raise more questions and
to see that there is probably not one comprehensive, single,
cause of the problem. The growing opinion seems to be that
all of the above named factors play a significant role in
addiction. What we are now trying to understand is how each
aspect may interact with the others. In this research, a new
component seems to have emerged that may link them. This is

the common denominator of **Stress**. The ordinary stress of everyday life is thought to play a significant role in the development of dependence, tolerance and finally addiction. Though scientists are still looking for biological markers in addiction, psychological and environmental factors are still thought to play a determining role in development of chemical dependence. With that in mind, we will take a look at stress and try to understand its role in alcohol and drug abuse.

What is stress? How does it work? What is its impact on health? What is its possible role in the development of addictions? These are the questions that need answering. And when we understand them, then, perhaps, we will be able to design more effective recovery programs.

Stress is a normal bodily response to demand. This demand may be internal or external. Our stress level reflects the amount of effort we expend adapting to to the demands of our lives. In simple terms, think of stress as your "cost of living index". The stress of day to day living is often not thought of as a problem. Research, however, has shown it to be far more damaging in the long run than major traumas such as job loss, death of a spouse, divorce or a major illness. When daily stress is combined with a major stressor, then a person becomes vulnerable. This is when we may see the development of a major illness or a person having serious stress symptoms.

Stress researchers have discovered a predictable cycle that occurs as a bodily and emotional response to interaction with our environment. Let us take a look now at this cycle as a basis for understanding its connection with drug and alcohol problems.

STAGE ONE: STIMULUS

Stage one of the stress response cycle is characterized by the alarm or trigger phase. Something, either internal or external, must be perceived as a trigger (stimulus). This signal may be anything: the alarm clock, driving to work, a conference with the boss, a too demanding work load, or each family member wanting some of your time. Any and all of these may combine to create a demand. A very simple definition of stress is, "when perceived demand is greater than our ability to respond." Demand creates arousal of the autonomic nervous system. When the nervous system is overly aroused, we experience tension; this is the body's way of getting ready to respond.

What determines whether an event is stressful? The major factor in stress is "Perception". Perception is the process of evaluating the incoming signal. How the incoming signal is translated or decoded for its meaning will determine both our bodily response and our emotional—behavioral response.

STAGE TWO: PERCEPTION

Perception or interpretation is the second phase in the stress response cycle. The cognitive component of stress is critical to the way we see things; the thoughts we have, the things we tell ourselves, and our expectations of the outcome of our actions. What is of importance when the alarm clock goes off or when our boss wants to talk to us, is how we interpret it. What is the emotional significance of these events?   The stress response is a very personal equation, because we are a uniquely perceiving subject.   If we are getting up to go on a fishing trip the alarm clock has one meaning; if we have to go in early to see a doctor because of a suspicious lump it has another.   Context and perception are critical to the stress response.   It all depends on perspective.   Perspective is a function of our own personal histories, our present environment, our emotional state and what has been happening overall in our lives.   Much more will be said about this as we go along.

STAGE THREE: ALARM

The third phase of the stress response cycle is the Alarm or arousal phase.   In this stage it is necessary to understand what is happening both physically, and psychologically.   If we have responded to the signal with alarm, that is to say, we have perceived a stimulus as a threat, then one component of our central nervous system is cued.   (see diagram 1)

This leads to a physical response of the body that is total and well integrated.   It is the body's tremendous adaptive abilities which are both a blessing and a curse: it is wonderfully equipped to handle emergencies.   Our body, once the alarm is signaled, is prepared to fight or to flee.   It is physiologically ready to perform complex tasks of adaptation. This is done by a series of glandular secretions and neurological activity which activates every system in the body.   In this sense, every bodily system is affected by the stress response.   The surge of adrenaline and other body hormones triggers the large muscles and expands the blood vessels; increases heart rate, respiration, oxygen and blood to the brain; stops digestion and increases the supply of energy which fuels the body. So here we are, primed for action!! All systems on red alert. Now what?

STAGE FOUR: COPING

At this point we usually engage in some form of activity to discharge the nervous system energy and return to normal. It is difficult as well as uncomfortable to just sit with this level of arousal in our bodies. We feel an urge to act. What is done next will determine our well-being. If we engage in effective problem solving, then we will experience relief, accomplishment, and satisfaction. If we do nothing, often we will continue to experience central nervous arousal (we're still pumped). If this condition becomes chronic, that is to say, if we run on a high level of stress for a long period of time, it will lead to both physical, as well as emotional exhaustion. This is the inevitable, natural consequence of a high stress lifestyle. Physical and emotional burnout are common sources of many stress related illnesses. The body is not made to remain on permanent emergency status.

It is at this point that chemical dependency may get a toehold. In other words, the danger is when we use chemicals as a part of our coping response. Because of our continual state of tension caused by the problems encountered in our lives, we are looking for relief from the tension. In fact, we may feel more frustrated and tense the harder we try. In short, we are unable to get rid of the tension and stress in

43

DIAGRAM 1

STRESS RESPONSE CYCLE

STRESSED = STRUGGLING TO COPE

SYMPATHETIC NERVOUS SYSTEM DOMINANCE

Step 1 **STIMULUS**

Either external or internal

Step 2 **APPRAISAL**

The stimulus is perceived and evaluated. We engage
in self—talk. We evaluate the demand. We determine
a response which is mediated on the basis of
thinking and feeling which leads to behavior aimed
at adaptation to perceived threat.

Step 3 **AROUSAL/FLIGHT OR FIGHT**

Physiological response — alarmed
Heart rate — increases
Respiration — increases
Endocrine system—secretes adrenaline
Vascular constriction
Muscular tension
Immune system - suppressed

Step 4 **BEHAVIORAL RESPONSE**

If demand exceeds ability to cope

self—esteem diminished
mood—depressed, anxious, or angry
a sense of helplessness or powerlessness
a lack of significance—relationships deteriorate

STRESS RESPONSE CYCLE

RELAXED = Optimum Well—being

Parasympathetic Nervous System Dominance

Step 1 **STIMULUS**

Either internal or external

Step 2 **APPRAISAL**

The stimulus is perceived and reevaluated. We engage in self—talk. Response is mediated as a function of thought process and feelings that lead to behavior.

Step 3 **AROUSAL/ NORMAL**

Physiological Response — Normal
Heart rate - Endocrine System—Normal
Respiration - Muscular System Normal
Vascular - Immune System — Normal

Step 4 **BEHAVIORAL RESPONSE/ADAPTIVE**

Self—esteem — maintained
Mood — optimistic — hopeful
Power — competent and successful
Significance — satisfactory relationships

our lives. Just as the central nervous system is made to respond to danger, it is also composed of those components that are responsive to pleasure. This nervous system is activated when we eat, have sex, are relaxing, or just having a good time.

The alarm nervous system and the pleasure nervous system inhibit each other; only one can be dominant at a time. If we are highly anxious, depressed, angry, frustrated, or feeling helpless, and take a drink, shoot up, smoke a joint, snort coke, or use some psycho-active substance, we turn off the stress system and turn on the pleasure centers in the brain. If this is done frequently, then an association is made between the drug and pleasure. Furthermore, we have *"learned"* a way to cope with tension.

This kind of learning may lead to the possibility of psychological dependence and an eventual build up of tolerance to the chemical. Everyone has the capacity for becoming psychologically dependent on anything that turns on pleasure and turns off pain.

Since everyone is different, the chemical of preference will be different. The length of time required to develop dependence and addiction is a function of several risk factors: each person's psychological makeup, biological predispositions, life situation, coping abilities, and the frequency, amount and type of substance used. Each person seems to have a preference for a chemical or blend of chemicals that give them that "certain feeling." In other words, use of psycho-active chemicals is a way of "self-medicating" a problem. The bottom line is that if using chemicals becomes a part of our coping strategies we have set in motion a very powerful set of circumstances that have very destructive and predictable consequences.

The solution appears to be in finding an adaptive way of coping, one that solves problems; we must find a response to the initial alarm, appraisal and arousal. Out of the vast array of possible responses to the situation, we must find one that will solve the problem. The goal is to solve the problem and return to normal levels of central nervous system arousal. Our responses usually fall into one of three categories: aggression (fight), flight (avoidance), or active coping (problem solving). Some engage in a fourth category, denial. This is, however, a basic form of avoidance. If we are not able to respond adaptively to the stressor, or do nothing, then we are likely to remain in a state of perpetual alarm. Our body continues producing the hormones to keep us prepared to fight or flee. In fact, we may intensify our coping attempts; increase our tension level, and be more frustrated. This can only go on for so long before we reach the exhaustion stage. Here is where the organism experiences the most damaging stress symptoms. They may be either physical or psychological. Usually, they are a combination of both.

STAGE FIVE: OUTCOME

This is the stage of outcome or resolution. It depends upon the success or failure of our coping strategies. If we have not coped successfully and allowed our bodies to return to a resting stage, then we begin to experience common symptoms such as chronic fatigue, irritability, apathy, emptiness, listlessness, head—aches, digestive disorders, muscle tension, high blood pressure, sleeplessness, anxiety, and depression. These symptoms are the signal, the natural consequence, of failing to cope with the demands of our lives. The result is feeling burned—out, helpless, empty, and overwhelmed.

The psychological consequences of chronic stress are usually depression, lowered self—esteem, and deteriorating relationships. Since we withdraw and have less energy to cope, we become resentful, and usually feel unappreciated and unloved. Our job performance also suffers from this same constellation of reactions.

Adequate, or functional responses to stress have, of course, quite the opposite effect on us emotionally, and psychologically. When a problem is dealt with in a manner that satisfies the demands of a current situation, there are natural consequences, as well. The first is relief. Secondly, we begin to experience the long term benefits of success: gains in confidence, increased feelings of competence, gains in self—esteem, and usually recognition and appreciation from others for accomplishments. Our bodies also benefit from success.

A happy person has a happy body. Our nervous system arousal is in the normal range and, in fact, may be experiencing more pleasure than pain. A further consequence of successful coping is the positive effect on our relationships. We feel better about ourselves; others respond to us positively and therefore we feel even better. It is a very positive, reinforcing cycle.

As one can readily see, this positive scene can shift dramatically if our response is not adequate to the presenting problem. When a person is presented with high demands, little time, and little power, the combination can be very stressful. In fact, this is the formula for stress: High Demand and Low Power = High Stress. For example, a very successful young man came to see me recently; he acknowledged a serious drinking problem.

He was a rising star in a corporation and all of his fellow executives were hard drinking, golf playing, fun loving drinkers. The problem was that he couldn't handle it. He had too many risk factors. (1) His father was an alcoholic, (2) his father was dying of cancer, (3) his job was overwhelming, (4) his wife was struggling with the loss of her mother due to cancer, and (5) all of his friends liked to party. He was fully aware that he was overwhelmed and that the only way he could keep going was by drinking. Too many risk factor!.

STRESS AND CHEMICALS

Let's look at this example to see what happens when the person uses a psycho—active chemical to cope with stress. Since he is experiencing chronic over—arousal of the nervous system, the chemicals serve to suppress this over— activity. He feels less tense, so the problems don't seem so bad after all. The chemicals have improved confidence and the euphoria may also affect the appraisal process; his thinking gets distorted and he feels like things aren't so bad after all. Besides that, he feels stronger, more confident, and optimistic. The energy returns and the problems seem manageable. When chemicals get incorporated into the stress—adaptation—response cycle regularly, a deadly and insidious dependence is acquired. "Better living through chemistry" is the slogan we have all heard in the stories told at A.A. meetings.

Learned behavior is acquired through reinforcement. Addictive behavior gets reinforced in three ways. First, ingesting chemicals when stressed causes the pleasure system to get turned on. By escaping pain and turning on pleasure, we have created a bond between the behavior and the consequence. A chain of behavior is being created. Stress = chemical use = pleasure = reinforcement = probability of doing this again. As second link in the chain is added through further reinforcement. Anything that allows us to escape pain is reinforcing. So using chemicals makes us feel better immediately and it also blots out the problem. A third and very powerful reinforcer may occur if we use chemicals with friends in situations that are highly pleasurable. This is social reinforcement, which is a very powerful shaper of behavior. If we gain friends, status, recognition, belonging and acceptance while using chemicals, we have created a potent reinforcement for addiction.

These, then, are some of the ways that chemical dependency is acquired. It is a response to stress that gets reinforced by providing pleasure, turning off pain, and gaining social reinforcement, as well. These powerful effects may lead a person to use with greater frequency. If this person has also grown up in an environment where alcohol and other chemicals were used regularly, another form of learning was taking place: social learning or modeling. We learn through imitation. If drinking was modeled as a form of problem solving and a means of family interaction, then this is also incorporated into the coping strategies of the potential addict. (See chart on Factors Involved)

In summary,the risk factors for addiction are several: (1) born and raised in an addicted family; (2) several family members are addicted; (3) personality factors such as low self—esteem and poor interpersonal relationships; (4) under high stress; (5) socially isolated; and (6) gains acceptance and status by using (social validation).

Using chemicals and being at risk create a potent basis for the development of a serious problem. As use increases, tolerance goes up and psychological dependence is acquired. As time passes, the use of chemicals becomes a greater part of the person's stress coping pattern. It becomes almost exclusively the means of getting by. Whatever adaptive functioning was being done, is gradually given up. The solution has now become the problem. It this pattern continues the acquired habits become harder to change and the destructive lifestyle becomes more consuming.

Recovery begins as we learn to recognize dysfunctional responses to stressful situations. In other words, find solutions that don't create more problems. Based on the model I have developed in this chapter, we may see several chances for

FACTORS INVOLVED IN ACQUISITION OF DEPENDENCY

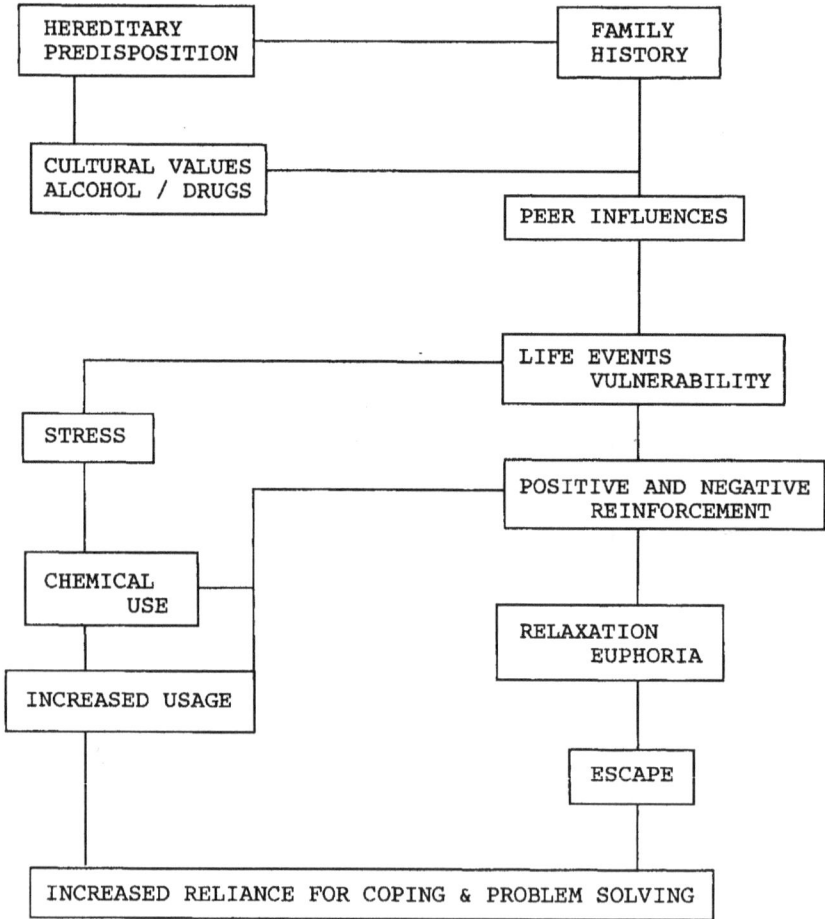

HEREDITARY PREDISPOSITION —— FAMILY HISTORY

CULTURAL VALUES ALCOHOL / DRUGS —— PEER INFLUENCES

LIFE EVENTS VULNERABILITY

STRESS

POSITIVE AND NEGATIVE REINFORCEMENT

CHEMICAL USE

RELAXATION EUPHORIA

INCREASED USAGE

ESCAPE

INCREASED RELIANCE FOR COPING & PROBLEM SOLVING

doing things differently. Although we don't have any control over the risk factors of our genetic makeup or our family history, we do have control over a number of other important factors.

The first opportunity for change and control in the stress cycle is at stage 1. Remember, this is the stage of the *trigger*. Many people are surprised to think we might have control in this area. That is because addicts are not accustomed to thinking of choice and control. "Things just seem to happen, I fell off the wagon." This is victim thinking. Another way to think of it is to react differently: *take stimulus control*. This is why it is important to get rid of all drug and alcohol paraphernalia. Get rid of the triggers. Another method of stimulus control is to stay out of bars, liquor stores, and avoid the pusher. It is difficult in our society to avoid all the triggers. Billboards, T.V. ads, friends, social situations, etc., all serve as powerful triggers. Avoid as many as you can and know what triggers you.

The second form of intervention or change and control is based on *perception*. This is our interpretation of the event. In the following chapters, we will focus on self-talk, faulty thinking, and ways of changing what we tell ourselves. Most of us engage in automatic thoughts and are not aware that we can change them or how they contribute to our problems. Changing our attitudes, self-talk and way we view addiction are all critical to recovery.

A third opportunity for coping occurs at the level of *physical arousal*. Again, most people are not aware of the fact that this can be changed. It is possible to learn to relax and change tension into more effective coping.

Finally, at the *behavioral response* level, there is often a need to learn more effective skills for problem solving. In the following chapters, we will systematically build effective coping skills that lead to better communication, management of powerful and difficult emotions, greater self—esteem, and enhanced abilities for intimacy and effective relationships. But for now, the task is to participate in the following exercises to continue gaining awareness.

One final observation must be made regarding stress and addiction. The use of mind and mood altering chemicals stimulate the activity of the Central Nervous System and mimic the effects of chronic stress by depleting the neurotransmitter substances which are critical to normal brain functioning. When a person stops using a chemical it takes a great deal of time for the Central Nervous System to return to normal. This aspect of recovery is known as Post Acute Withdrawal Syndrome (PAWS). Recovery is further complicated by the cessation of use because the stress level goes up as the user begins the process of getting straight. It is no wonder so many struggle at this point; increased stress, psychological and physiological vulnerability and lack of a chemical crutch. More will be said about this in the chapter on relapse prevention.

The following exercises are designed to increase awareness by teaching you self—monitoring skills. Awareness is necessary to build better coping skills.

Learning to cope with stress means to learn what our stressors are, how to turn off the distressing arousal, implement appropriate coping strategies, and change our thoughts about the stressors. In short, interventions may be either physical, mental, or behavioral.

In sections to come we will focus more on specific coping skills and have ample time for practice and reinforcement.

CHAPTER 2
STRESS AND CHEMICAL DEPENDENCY
EXERCISE 1
Multi—Dimensional Life Stress Index

A Life—Style Measure

Directions for use:

Stress is the overall effect of the cost of living. It is the amount of energy that is needed to effectively cope with our lives. Since our lives are complex patterns of interrelated dimensions, it is important to evaluate these dimensions to determine the amount of stress they may be causing. By looking at each one independently, we may be able to determine the major areas of both strength, as well as stress. Examine each dimension by allowing yourself to see how deeply you feel. Sit quietly—let yourself be immersed in the dimension under examination. Pay very close attention to the overall impression and the major feeling you have as you let yourself explore each dimension, one at a time. Continue doing this with each area. You may also want to write down any particular thoughts or impressions that come to you as you examine each aspect of your life. Now, on a scale of 0—10 give a score to each area.

0 is totally dissatisfied

10 is very comfortable

After you have examined each area, add up your scores and divide by 10. You now have an average of your life satisfaction. What are the strong areas? What are the weak and perhaps the most stressful?

Make note of these areas.

CHAPTER 2

STRESS AND CHEMICAL DEPENDENCY

EXERCISE 2

MULTI—DIMENSIONAL LIFE STRESS INDEX

		SCORE
(1)	Self—esteem	_____
(2)	Vocation	_____
(3)	Interpersonal relationships	_____
(4)	Primary family network (marriage)	_____
(5)	Family of origin (mother, father)	_____
(6)	Financial Conditions	_____
(7)	Life—space (living environment)	_____
(8)	Meaning dimension (Religion, values, personal philosophy of life) Experience your life as having meaning, purpose, and significance.	_____
(9)	Pleasure (recreation—hobbies, creativity, life enjoyment)	_____
(10)	Physical health	_____

TOTAL _____

CHAPTER 2

STRESS AND CHEMICAL DEPENDENCY

EXERCISE 3

Daily Stress Baseline

The daily stress baseline work sheet is designed to establish the average daily level of stress experienced day in and day out: this is what is meant by *baseline.* By becoming aware of stress at the moment of occurrence, you will be able to notice how much stress you are experiencing; become aware of the connections between the event (stressor) and your stress level; and observe what you do immediately following a stressful situation.

The importance of this exercise is to examine relationships between events, your subjective states, physiological reactions, behavioral responses and habits. The goal is to help you to see patterns of behavior emerging that perhaps you were not aware were occurring.

Once you have begun to notice certain relationships that occur frequently in your life it will become possible to change your behavior to make it more effective in dealing with these stressors. We call this *self-monitoring or tracking.*

CHAPTER 2
STRESS AND CHEMICAL DEPENDENCY
EXERCISE 4

Directions for use:

The purpose of the daily stress work sheet is to focus upon everyday activities and to examine them from a new perspective. Often we are not aware of how much energy they take from us. It is not the major traumas of our lives that wear us down. It is the average, everyday stress level that is an important indicator of the amount of stress with which we are confronted.

STRESS LEVEL: Imagine a stressometer much like a speedometer, 0 is resting and 100 is maximum stress. Give each activity a rating during the day that causes your stress level to exceed a score of 40. Do not record those incidents that do not exceed 40.

INCIDENT: Describe what occurred. What happened?

BEHAVIORAL OBSERVATIONS: Now describe what you did, said, thought and felt. Did this increase or decrease your stress level?

AVERAGE DAILY STRESS LEVEL: Add up all the scores and divide by the number of events.

MOST STRESSFUL ACTIVITY: What was it?

PREDOMINANT MOOD AT END OF THE DAY: How do you generally feel after each day?

STRESS ASSESSMENT DIARY				
TIME	STRESS LEVEL	BEHAVIORAL EVENT	COPING MECHANISM	OUTCOME

AVERAGE DAILY STRESS LEVEL =

MOST STRESSFUL ACTIVITY =

PREDOMINANT MOOD AT END OF DAY =

CHAPTER 2

EXERCISE 5

STRESS AND CHEMICAL DEPENDENCY
QUIET MIND—QUIET BODY

Quieting the mind requires practice and discipline. Most of us suffer from an internal noise problem that serves the purpose of keeping us mentally and physically agitated. One technique that has been found to be very effective for this malady is Meditation. This, for some, brings to mind the behavior of yogi's, mystics, and rooms full of chanting Tibetan monks.

In reality, meditation is a very sound technique for quieting the mind and regulating the body. Its benefits include: lowered blood pressure, increased relaxation, improved mood, less troubled thoughts, and greater calmness. You don't need to go to a temple to study with a yoga, or be a religious initiate to learn to meditate. It does, however, take time, practice, and consistency of effort.

In this exercise you will be instructed in only one form of meditation. There are many different ways to go about it. This exercise is found in many different cultures.

The goal of this exercise is to learn to observe your thoughts and to let them flow without judging them. By learning the technique of detached observation, you will learn to let go of thoughts and feelings which, if hung onto, will cause great distress.

MEDITATION

1. Begin by sitting quietly where you won't be disturbed.

2. Sit quietly—let your mind focus on the task at hand.

3. Close your eyes, take a deep breath, imagine yourself sitting by a slow moving stream.

4. Let your mind be quiet, if a thought comes, let it be like a log, let it drift on down the stream of consciousness. Don't hang onto it. Return to watching the water flow. Just wait quietly, mind empty. If a noise disturbs you, let it flow in and out, don't grab onto it. Just sit quietly, watching the stream, letting thoughts flow away.

5. Practice this meditation for 10 minutes a day for two weeks. If it helps and you like it, then do it whenever you need to calm your mind. Remember, a calm mind calms the body.

6. Listen to instructional tape #2 on Meditation.

CHAPTER 2
STRESS AND CHEMICAL DEPENDENCY
EXERCISE 6
RELAXATION

There are basically four things required to achieve a state of deep relaxation. This is the antidote for tension. The first is a calm and quiet environment. It should be free of interruptions and noise. Secondly, allow yourself plenty of time to get relaxed. This is very important, few people give themselves the luxury of sitting down and relaxing. It requires serious commitment. Thirdly, to relax you must quiet the mind. This requires effort and frequent practice. Finally, there must be a systematic approach to relaxation that is practiced on a regular basis until it becomes a well learned response that can be called forth at will. It should take about two weeks of continuous practice for this to become a part of you. Fifteen minutes a day will lead to mastery of this technique.

Listen to instructional tape # 1 Relaxation.

CHAPTER 2

STRESS AND CEMICAL DEPENDENCY

EXERCISE 6

RELAXATION

* Begin the exercise in a quiet and comfortable place—free from distractions and interruptions.
Give yourself one half hour to deeply relax.

* Begin the exercise the same way every time, by giving yourself the relaxation cue. By doing this you are conditioning a relaxation response to the cue.

* Begin by taking a long—slow—deep breathe. On the exhale tell yourself to relax. Now take another one slowly—relax. Now another one. Breathing is the key to relaxation——you cannot be relaxed and anxious at the same time.

* Begin relaxing your muscles by systematically tensing each muscle group and then releasing the tension.

* From this point breathing is deep, regular and comfortable and your eyes are closed.

* Tighten the muscles of your forehead like you are frowning. Hold the muscles tight, then on the exhale release all the tension.

* Next tighten the muscles of your jaw (like biting down) then release the tightness again as you exhale.

* Tighten your neck muscles. Hold and then relax as you exhale.

* Now your shoulders. First roll the shoulders forward. Relax as you exhale.

* Then push your shoulders back, relaxing the shoulders and letting them droop as you exhale. To relax your chest, interlace your fingers and push the palms together—let yourself go limp and let your hands fall as you exhale. Then, with fingers laced, pull apart again letting your arms fall as you breathe out. Pretend you are lifting a table, hold the tension, very rigid, then let all relax, arms again fall as you exhale. Tense your stomach, make it as tight as you can— slowly relax. Arch your lower back and maintain the tightness. Relax that muscle group on the out—breath.

65

* Tighten the front of your thighs, then relax.

* Now the back of your thighs. "Feel the tension melt away as you breathe out."

* Tighten your calves by pointing your toes, then relax.

* Create tension in your shins by flexing your foot, then go calm and quiet.

* Lastly, arch your foot as if you're holding on floppy shoes. Breathe out and relax your soles. You are physically relaxed from the top of your head to the soles of your feet.

* Keep your eyes closed and enjoy the quietness. Now extend the calmness to your thoughts.

* Quiet your mind by picturing an enjoyable spot. Imagine in intricate detail all sights, sounds, scents, and the feel of this serene scene. Now let the scene go. Just sit, allow your mind to be blank. Concentrate on your breathing. If thoughts come in, let them vanish, don't fight them. Now that you are completely relaxed, feel the difference between now and when you started. Practice this exercise daily. You will become adept at it after 10 or 12 practice sessions. Once you have practiced systematic relaxation you can elicit the relaxation response on cue. Just take a deep breath, tell yourself to relax and let your mind go quiet. Do this whenever you find yourself tense, anxious, or upset.

CHAPTER 2

STRESS AND CHEMICAL DEPENDENCY

EXERCISE 7

Stress Awareness Checklist

The first step in changing your stress response begins with awareness of signs of stress. Your body is an excellent and reliable barometer of your stress level. In this exercise the goal is to develop a bodily awareness of stress. I call this the organ recital or body scan.

In the space provided indicate how often each of the following happens to you either when you are experiencing stress, or following exposure to a stressor. Please respond to each item indicating a number ranging from 0–5. Use the following frequency scale.

0 = Never

1 = Rarely

2 = Every few months

3 = Every few weeks

4 = Once or twice a week

5 = Daily

Bodily System Review (organ recital)

Cardiovascular

_____ Heart Pounding

_____ Heart racing or beating erratically

_____ Cold hands or feet

_____ Pain or tightness in chest

_____ Subtotal

Head

_____ Headache

_____ Dizziness

_____ Blurred vision

_____ Visual disturbance with nausea and throbbing pain

_____ Subtotal

Respiratory

_____ Rapid, erratic or shallow breathing

_____ Shortness of breath

_____ Asthma attack

_____ Difficulty in speaking because of poor breath control

_____ Sighing or labored breathing

_____ Subtotal

Gastrointestinal

_____ Upset stomach, nausea or vomiting

_____ Constipation

_____ Sharp abdominal pains

_____ Loss of appetite

_____ Subtotal

Musculoskeletal

_____ Persistent neck and shoulder pain

_____ Lower back pain

_____ Muscular tremors or hands shaking

_____ Arthritis

_____ Subtotal

Skin

_____ Acne

_____ Dandruff

_____ Excessive sweating

_____ Hair falling out in large amounts

_____ Excessive dryness of skin or hair

_____ Subtotal

Immune System

_____ Allergy flare up

_____ Catching colds frequently

_____ Skin rash

_____ Sinus reactions

_____ Get sick and can't seem to get over it

_____ Subtotal

Metabolism

_____ Increased appetite

_____ Increased craving for sweets

_____ Increased craving for tobacco or alcohol

_____ Racing thoughts

_____ Difficulty in sleeping

_____ Feelings of apprehension, anxiety, or nervousness

_____ Listless, apathetic, tired or depressed

_____ Subtotal

_____ **Total score: Add all subtotals**

Understanding your score

0—40 **Mild stress symptoms.** No problem
A score in this range indicates a low level of
physical stress symptoms thereby predicting a low
probability of psychosomatic illness in the near
future.

40—80 **Moderate physical stress symptoms** This is an
average score indicating most people fall into this
category. There is likelihood of some susceptibility
to psychosomatic illness but no immediate illness in
the near future.

80—150 **Excessive physical stress symptoms** A score in
this range indicates a serious frequency of symptoms.
It is strongly indicated that you are headed for one
or more episodes of illness in the near future. You
should take immediate action to reduce your stress.

CHAPTER 2

STRESS AND CHEMICAL DEPENDENCY

EXERCISE 8

The Feedback Loop

Now that you have reviewed and assessed the functioning of all of your major biological systems it is time to shift the focus to awareness of specific areas of tension that you may be experiencing now. This exercise is like Bio—Feedback in that it is designed to develop a feedback loop between your body, behavior, and consciousness. It differs from biofeedback only in that we are trying to create the awareness without hooking you up to a feedback machine. The goals are: **(1)** to develop the capacity for awareness of bodily signs of stress. **(2)** the ability to translate these distress signals into meaningful information, **(3)** and finally, to be able to formulate new response patterns based on the information gained in the feedback loop. The loop, then would look like this: **awareness————analysis————action.**

Bodily Awareness Training

Begin by sitting quietly.

Close your eyes.

Quiet your mind.

Take a deep breath.

Focus on your body.

Notice your most immediate sensations.

What part of your body are you most aware of?

What is the sensation? Tension? Pain? Fatigue?

What is the overall feeling tone in your body?

BODILY AWARENESS TRAINING

What is your energy level? Now, shift your focus to a specific area. Let us start with the head and work down.

HEAD

Any pain? What are the muscles in your face doing? Focus your attention. Are they tense? Relaxed? Tight? Loose? How about your jaw? Do you grind your teeth? Do you clench your jaw and bite things back? What is your facial mask like? What do others see in your face? Angry? Worried? Fearful? Cynical? Sad?

Notice that these bodily sensations are usually accompanied by thoughts and feelings. What are they? Jot these down in a notebook. Take a moment to record anything that you become aware of as you focus on your bodily sensations. Sometimes fleeting images, thoughts, and barely perceptible feelings may gradually come together into a perception that will tell you what this pain or distress is all about. Writing it down without editing; it may bring things together into a new way of looking at yourself and deepen your understanding. Now, proceed to your neck and shoulder area and repeat the same process. This is a particularly significant area because it is where we often "guard against attack" so we carry a lot of tension here. This guarding is a kind of body armor. A sign of being uptight. Just pay attention to the sensations in your body.

BODILY AWARENESS TRAINING

Do it again with your chest. Any pain? Tightness? How is your heart beating? Is your pulse rapid? How is your breathing? Is it high and shallow? Try taking a deep breath from deep in the chest and diaphragm. Go on down to your stomach and abdomen. How does it function. Do you localize your pain, fear, tension or anger here? Do you allow things to eat at you? Do you swallow your anger? How do your bowels work? Are you a tight ass? (constipated) Do you feel shitty? (diarrhea) Is life a pain in the rectum? (hemorrhoids). Notice how often our language may speak of bodily processes in symbolic ways and how this language may show up as bodily symptoms. Examples: Broken heart. Choking rage. Being choked up (grief).

Can you think of your own body language and how it may show up in your speech? Where do you localize your pain or emotions? Pay attention to your lower back. Many people carry tension here. Finally, continue to scan the rest of your body using this same format. Once you have done this, take a moment to process the sensations and write down any final thoughts that may occur to you. Now it is time to put it all together in a new way. Stand before a full length mirror. Look at yourself. Notice your body language. Look at your face, your posture, how you characteristically dress. How do you stand? What do you see? How do you feel about this person standing before you? What do you think others see when they look at you? Now, spend some time writing down reflections from this exercise. Describe you, your self-image; how others see you. Did you come across any new information? Which area seems to be the most distressing? Look back at your own history and see if you can get in touch with how others treated your body. How did this one area come to be the focus of distress? Did other family members have the same symptom?

This exercise, in order to become a meaningful tool for stress awareness, should be practiced frequently for maximum benefit. Gradually you will notice that you will be in contact with your body in a new and comfortable way. This feedback loop will help you live with greater awareness and joy as you are free to feel all of your bodily sensations.

You are your body. So, enjoy the sensations, treat yourself well. Get to know you through this channel of sensations.

CHAPTER 2

STRESS AND CHEMICAL DEPENDENCY

FURTHER READING

Benson, Herbert. The Relaxation Response. New York: William Morrow, 1975.

Davis, Martha. Eshelman, Elizabeth, and Mckay, Mathew. The Relaxation and Stress Reduction Workbook Third Edition. Oakland, CA: New Harbinger Pub., 1988.

Mckay, Mathew, Davis, Martha, Fanning, Patrick. Thoughts and Feelings. Richmond, Ca: New Harbinger Pub., 1981.

Selye, Hans. The Stress of Life. New York: McGraw Hill Book Co., 1978.

NOTES

WHO AM I?

The way is not without danger. Everything good is costly, and the development of personality is one of the most costly. It is a matter of saying yes to oneself, as taking oneself as the most serious of tasks, of being conscious of everything one does, and keeping it before one's eyes...truly a task that taxes us to the utmost.

Carl Jung

Identity, that core sense of self, is the most central factor in determining the course of our lives. We live out our sense of identity in numerous and complex ways: in relationships, career choices, our relationship to ourselves, and as we strive to fulfill our dreams. Living with a sense of satisfaction and fulfillment is the most challenging experience any of us will face. Every day, as our daily journey unfolds, our identity is at risk. When we are unable to live our lives in accordance with our basic identity we develop distress.

If the distress reaches very uncomfortable levels over time we may reach a crisis of identity. This is manifested in many different ways. Some of my clients have stated it this way, "I don't know who I am," others say, "I feel so lost and confused, I can't seem to find myself." When we feel threatened in our identity, we feel intense anxiety because our core self is at stake. When we feel unable to control our world, helpless to meet basic needs, or be the kind of person we have envisioned, despair or depression may result. Many of our difficulties in life are a result of how we try to manage these threats to our identity.

Crises of identity have reached epidemic proportions because of the kind of culture we live in. Large, industrialized, anonymous, cultures lend themselves to impersonality and lack of intimacy. These do not create the conditions which make for sound identity formation. So, instead of people being grounded in a solid sense of identity and community, they live with uncertainty and are continually looking for ways to feel significant, purposeful, and meaningfully connected to others.

Maintaining our sense of identity in a complex, accelerated culture has recently been chronicled in a movie called, "Grand Canyon." The characters are depicted as frightened, lost and harassed; all looking for that same thing, certainty and control over their lives. As they experience all of the catastrophes of daily life in the big city, earthquakes, violence, divorce, death, financial insecurity, and career disappointment, they struggle to love and get connected in some meaningful way.

To have a sense of identity means in part to be somebody to someone. We gain a large portion of our identity from our attachments and relationships. Because of the great deal of anxiety associated with finding ourselves, this has come to be known as the age of identity. It is a preoccupation which is not only chronicled in the movies, but it is also reflected in songs and other forms of popular culture.

Identity and various forms of crises have been a professional as well as a personal preoccupation for many years. My fascination has led me to investigate the complex roots of identity. To really understand identity, I have concluded, one has to look at sociology, anthropology, psychology and mythology. All of this is filtered through our present culture and finds its focus in the lives of unique individuals. Because we are so complex and preoccupied, most people do not think too much about the issue until a problem develops. It only becomes a problem when we can't seem to sustain our identity. Then, as our anxiety or despair mounts, we struggle to find solutions. These problems are often manifested symptomatically in broken relationships, inability to find satisfaction in life, a sense of emptiness, boredom, or restlessness. Increased alcohol and drug consumption may be used to quiet the uneasy feeling that something is missing. This occurs when life stops making sense and the things which once were satisfying, no longer mean anything. In a crisis of identity, there is a growing sense of disappointment captured in the poignant phrase, "is this all there is?"

Identity, then, is that particular, very personal, window on the world which makes a person totally unique. Our identity is like a thumb print. Each of us views the world from a completely subjective vantage point. The vantage point of "I". This is what is meant by *Identity.*

I am often asked, "Why bother trying to understand all of this stuff?" I have so many people say to me, "Oh, that happened a long time ago, it doesn't bother me now, I have forgotten all about that." This too easily slights the importance of identity as an issue. It is a form of denial which would write off early experiences because they may in fact be too painful to face. My intent in this section is to help readers understand the importance of childhood experiences as they work their way out through life stages, and perhaps the role they play in the development of chemical dependency.

As we look at the origins of identity, some material may evoke painful memories. For example, as a graduate student I read Erik Erikson's book on identity crisis, and as I completed it I realized I felt very depressed. As I took a look at those feelings, I recognized that the pervasive feeling was failure; that I had not achieved any sense of lasting identity. It was as though I had failed every developmental stage. I hope that for the reader this material may prove a helpful way of beginning the quest for self understanding and that it will become a tool for healing. I will leave it to you to draw your own conclusions about the connection your childhood has to your current behavior.

In my view of psychology the idea of Identity is central, it is the foundation for everything. Identity, as I define it, is that core, organizing, and determining sense of self which governs all of our behavior. All of the things with which I identify determine what I care about, what I strive for and ultimately what I value. How I identify myself, who I say that I am, has many levels. Just as you answer the question "who am I?" in many different ways.

These dimensions vary from intensely personal feelings of my inner self to the superficial public persona of being a Laker fan or a devotee of vanilla ice cream. To repeat, identity is the core of human personality, it is like the floor plan of a house. Some of our identity is very conscious. I can identify myself as a male Caucasian, a father, a mental health professional, an American, a Laker Fan, a Californian, etc. I can go on with my preference in cars, clothing, food, politics, hobbies and music. The more I reveal about myself, the more you, the reader, begin to form certain kinds of impressions and opinions about who I am.

For an overview of the factors contributing to identity, refer to the Origins of Identity Chart.

As you fill in the blanks with your ideas about me, you make a judgment. This is based on your own experiences, your preferences, prejudices, and stereotypes about all of my qualities. We call these preferences, the things with which we identify, *identifications*. These identifications are things, ideas, groups of people, causes, or values that we have taken in and made a part of ourselves. Identity, then, is the sum of all of our identifications. This forms the basis for our way of looking at and interacting with our world. In this sense identity is a Gestalt. This is a word that means a whole. In psychology the term Gestalt means "a whole that is greater than the sum of its parts." A person's Identity is a Gestalt, we are the whole which is greater than the sum of our parts. All ofthe parts are interdepdndent and together they form the basis of our personality.

As I mentioned, many of these identifications are conscious. Many, however, are not. In my work as a therapist, I spend a great deal of time helping people become aware of those parts of themselves of which they may not be aware. For example, a young man with whom I have worked for a long time came in the other day and was totally enraged. As we explored his feelings he discovered that he had repressed many very deeply felt feelings for his father who was an alcoholic. At the bottom of his rage was a great hurt at having never felt loved or appreciated and having been verbally, and emotionally abused. When his father criticized him the other day, it brought all of the old wounds to the surface. In this client's history there are alcoholic grandparents on both sides of the family as well. In addition, my patients father was emotionally abused by his alcoholic father. Neither of my patient's parents were effective in providing love, security, or the emotional climate for developing healthy identity. My client had identified with a father who was cold and abusive and a mother who was overprotective and anxious. This left him feeling responsible for his mother's happiness and together they formed an angry alliance against his father. In identifying with his father, my client was treating himself the way his father treated him. Hence, he was angry at himself, his father, and feeling guilty for wanting to break away from his mother. He was also, quite understandably, feeling like a hurt and unloved child.

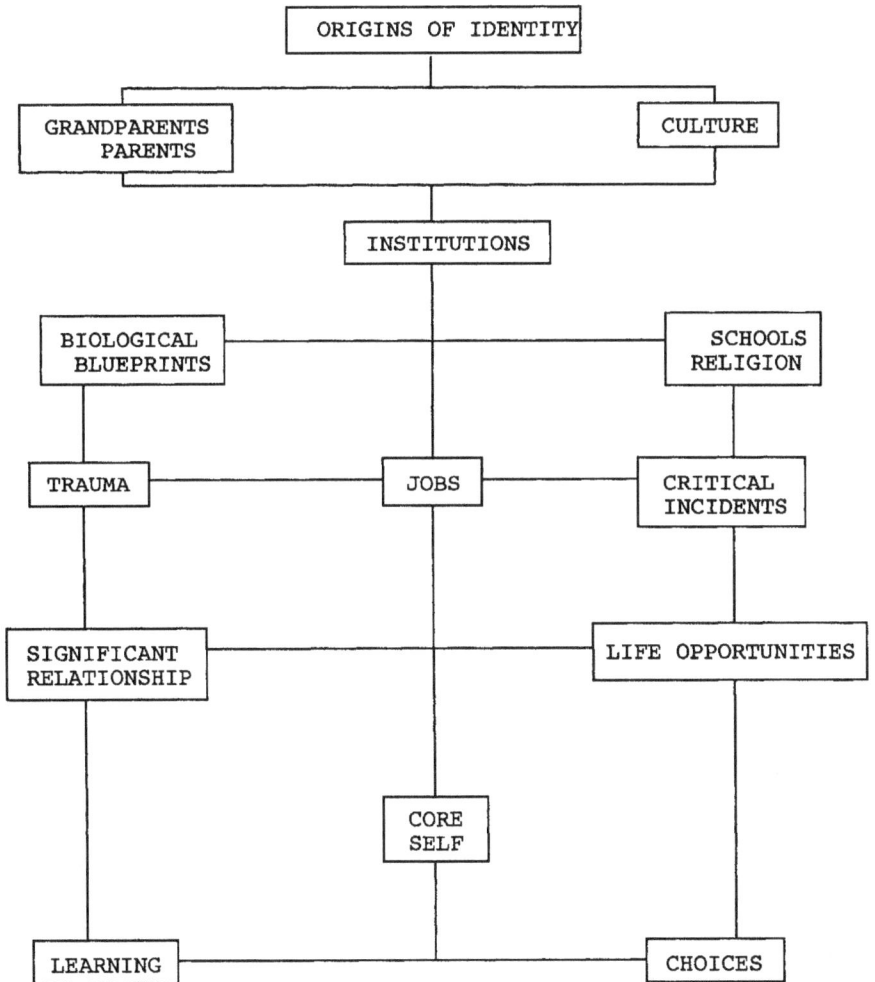

```
                    ┌─────────────────────┐
                    │ ORIGINS OF IDENTITY │
                    └─────────────────────┘
                               │
        ┌──────────────────────┴──────────────────────┐
┌─────────────────┐                          ┌─────────────┐
│  GRANDPARENTS   │                          │   CULTURE   │
│    PARENTS      │                          └─────────────┘
└─────────────────┘                                 │
        └──────────────────────┬──────────────────────┘
                    ┌──────────────────┐
                    │   INSTITUTIONS   │
                    └──────────────────┘
                               │
┌─────────────────┐                          ┌─────────────┐
│   BIOLOGICAL    │──────────────────────────│   SCHOOLS   │
│   BLUEPRINTS    │                          │  RELIGION   │
└─────────────────┘                          └─────────────┘
        │                      │                     │
┌──────────────┐      ┌──────────────┐      ┌──────────────┐
│    TRAUMA    │──────│     JOBS     │──────│   CRITICAL   │
└──────────────┘      └──────────────┘      │  INCIDENTS   │
        │                      │            └──────────────┘
┌─────────────────┐                          ┌──────────────────┐
│   SIGNIFICANT   │──────────────────────────│ LIFE OPPORTUNITIES│
│  RELATIONSHIP   │                          └──────────────────┘
└─────────────────┘                                 │
        │              ┌──────────────┐             │
        │              │     CORE     │             │
        │              │     SELF     │             │
        │              └──────────────┘             │
┌──────────────┐              │            ┌──────────────┐
│   LEARNING   │──────────────┴────────────│   CHOICES    │
└──────────────┘                           └──────────────┘
```

This case example illustrates some of the ways that our personal histories influence our current behavior. My intent is to demonstrate the way the historical roots of identity play a role in the ordinary drama of every day experience.

With this in mind, let us take a look at the structure of identity and how it develops. As we go along, I encourage you to keep a note pad and pen handy, jot down any memories or thoughts that might come to you as we explore early childhood experiences. Make this an opportunity for self—exploration. Try not to censor your thoughts or feelings. Just notice them, let them flow. These experiences are neither good nor bad. When you judge your feelings you tend to label them good or bad and therefore inhibit the flow of feelings and create guilt for feeling the way you do.

The Structure of Identity

When we are born, we come into the world with the potential of our biological heritage. What happens to us after that is a function of learning, culture, and the skill of our caretakers. The ability of our parents to protect, nurture, love, and foster our self—esteem determines, in large measure, who we become. In this complex process the adults around us form the social and emotional environment in which we learn the skills of adaptation and survival, Becoming human, like no other species, is largely social learning; very little is driven by instinct.

Through the bonds of attachment, formed from the first seconds after birth, we encounter the rich, complex, cultural heritage of which our family is one small unit. Whether this drama unfolds in a small town in the South, an industrial city in the Northeast, a Midwestern farming community, or a California suburb influences the direction identity takes. These racial, ethnic, economic and social class factors play significant roles in shaping identity: the sum of them is our unique self.

The story of identity unfolds through the interaction of the individual with the world as presented in the family. Let us look briefly, at some of the processes involved in this transmittal of culture.

Our grand entrance on the stage is quite important. The first dimension of identity, *Attachment,* begins here at the moment we are greeted by our caretakers. The quality of greeting is crucial to further development. This emotional bonding continues onward throughout the life cycle and is largely responsible for the measure of happiness we experience in our interpersonal relationships. Bonding is essentially what makes it possible for us to become human. This attachment bond, the emotional link between infant and care—giver is vital to the survival of all infants. The quality and nature of the attachment bond is the prototype for all other relationships.

The ability to have satisfactory and lasting relationships is the key to well—being and success in life. The encounters of the first four years of life form the basis for what is learned about the world of people and how we fit into that world. The ability to give and receive love, the ability to trust, our feelings of worthiness and autonomy are all acquired in these formative attachments. If trauma or dysfunction occurs in this developmental stage many people spend the rest of their lives in a form of compulsive reenactment of this stage. In short we spend the rest of our lives trying to get it right.

In sum, the attachment bond is the cornerstone of human personality. The emotional well—being of all children hinges on it. This world of relationships is the vehicle; the means by which everything else is learned. To be human is to be in relationships. The manner in which we establish and maintain our relationships is one mark of our identity.

A second dimension of identity is the *Mind*. Our rational or *Cognitive* functioning serves to separate us from all other species. Cognitive development is paartially dependent on our biological heritage; but is also strongly influenced by environment. The quality of environment may influence I.Q. by as much as twenty points, or in the case of severe abuse or deprivation even greater. What is remarkable about infancy is that a naive infant is introduced into the big buzzing world of sight, sound and physical objects and is able to learn a language in two years with no previous training or experience.

Like a miniature scientist, the infant begins to decode symbols, put relationships, objects, and people all together in a sensible whole. With the beginning of language comes the ability to think, to manipulate objects, and most importantly to communicate wants and needs to others. With communication we join the human family, we overcome our isolation and participate in social interactions. Thus, we come to belong through communication and bonding. The child, through constant interaction, play, physical activity, and manipulating physical objects, is forming ideas about the very nature of the family, and the larger universe as well.

These ideas about reality are called *"schemata"*. Think of them as maps in the mind. When you go for a walk in your neighborhood, or even move about in your house at night, you do so by having learned the lay of the land. These memory blueprints (schemata) become highly organized as more and more information is acquired. They form the basis of our interaction with the world. There are many kinds of schemata that form in infancy and childhood. One of the first maps is the "mother—schema". Another is the "self—schema". A different and more general kind of schema pertains to the physical world in which the task for the child is to learn object constancy.

The game a child plays by throwing things on the floor is an exercise in physics. The child is learning that just because he can't see it, it doesn't mean that it is gone forever. When mother goes into another room it doesn't mean she has abandoned him. These are important concepts because they form the basis of a stable and organized world.

The child is building up a perceptual—cognitive world of rules, expectations, relationships, and meanings. This world is built up through language and experience. A basic belief system, a cognitive world, is growing with the self—schema at the very center, holding it all together. And this self continues to develop throughout the lifespan.

Thinking, at first, is very primitive and concrete. Gradually, progressing through infancy, childhood, and adolescence, thought processes become more abstract. As adults, we are capable of mastering and manipulating objects without having to touch or see them. What is important for our purposes here is the concept of *Cognitive-schemata.* These are the crucial ideas that form the basis of self, others, and life in general. These maps form the content of our inner dialogue, our expectations about the world, and the way we perceive people. These ideas become an inner dialogue, a commentary about what is going on about us. This self-talk leads to emotions and behavior. It is what governs all behavior. It is the enduring paradigm which filters all experience.

To illustrate the function of the "self-other schema," let us say that through interaction with an anxious and overprotective mother and an angry and critical father, a child learns not to trust himself, to fear the world, and that other people are angry, critical, and dangerous—not to be trusted. The self schema becomes, "I'm no good." Imagine how this set of ideas and expectations about the self and the world gets played out in early childhood, and continues on into adulthood. The child goes to school, rather fearfully separating from mother, avoids people, is afraid to tackle problems, expects to fail and expects disapproval. He is shy, and stays to himself.

The child becomes labeled a poor student, doesn't receive much praise or success, which confirms the basic beliefs he has about himself; the shame and feelings of inferiority become reinforced through daily confirmation. He does not see people as helpful or supportive so, his social reality also gets reinforced. Hence, we see how the beliefs about self, the world and other people become "self—fulfilling prophecies". We get what we expect. As if to say, "I knew it all along." This is what we tell ourselves in our inner dialogue, the language of the self, learned through interaction with significant others. We relate to ourselves with the words and attitudes of mom and dad, brothers and sisters, and these become the self—schema that is the core of identity.

This is why it is crucial to understand the role of cognitive development in the formation of identity. Many of these ideas do not serve us well as adults. Another example comes to mind. Several years ago I was working with a man who was a professor at a major university. He had a Ph.D. from an Ivy League school. He came to see me because of severe depression. He was not functioning at his job, nor was he able to carry out ordinary daily activities. The thing that seemed to cause his depression was the fact that he was coming up for tenure.

It is interesting how success can also trigger depression. The problem was that his inner world did not match his outer success. Inwardly, my client perceived himself as inadequate. He had managed to get by in life by fooling others. In other words, he did not believe he deserved the promotion. He stated to me that he was living in fear that they would find out he was an impostor. He had made it to the big leagues, but felt like a little leaguer.

When such a discrepancy between the self—schema and the outer world exists, this creates tremendous inner tension. This may precipitate a crisis of identity. Anxiety and depression are usually symptomatic of such gaps between the inner and the publicly seen self. Some, in order to fend off a collapse of the self, may turn to alcohol or other mind altering chemicals. By turning off the pain and creating a false sense of euphoria the feelings of inferiority may be masked and the anxiety of being found out may be quelled for a while.

As can readily be seen, ideas about ourselves and our relationships always have a strong feeling component. This is the third dimension of identity: *Feelings.* All human experience is accompanied by feelings. Feelings are to the psyche what pain is to the body. Feelings provide the tone quality to experience. They make life exhilarating, joyful, or unbearable and full of anguish. For many people it is this area of life that is so troublesome and results in many forms self—destructive behavior.

What we do with our feelings and how we experience them is, again, largely the product of learning and social experience. Though we are born with the capacity and potential to feel love, joy, fear, rage, frustration, and sadness, each particular society has both written and unwritten rules about the expression of feelings. Certain feelings are taboo; some may be shown in private, some are permissible in public, some are acceptable between men and women but not between men and menor women and women etc..

Feelings that are taboo may cause shame and guilt for those who experience them. For example, a very common belief in our culture is that only women should cry. Men are taught from a very early age that tears are a sign of weakness. This may lead to some feelings that are extremely painful being repressed or totally blocked. As we develop we learn ways of handling feelings in order to relate to others as well as to shield ourselves from our own internal pain. These are called *defense mechanisms.*

We will be exploring various kinds of feelings and the role that defense mechanisms play in greater depth and detail as we go along. Feelings are mentioned here to emphasize their importance to the development and functioning of identity. The role that feelings play in the individual's life depend, in large measure, upon the emotional climate of the family of origin. How we handle feelings now and how feelings are integrated into one's personality are a good measure of psychological maturity.

Generally, the kinds of feelings that are troublesome, which feelings are blocked, or whether one is entirely governed by feelings markers of our identity: our personal style. People recognize us as warm or as cold and insensitive, ruthless, angry, or a fearful person.

Feelings are intricately related to the other areas of personality in very powerful ways. Fear may be associated with intimacy, with aggression, or anything that serves as a

threat.   Rage may be experienced in a variety of ways:
frustration, competition, shame, or depression. All of these
have a root in anger.

Attachment, thinking, feeling and behavior are all a
deeply interdependent product of complex learning experiences.
As a whole, they reflect our personal style in relationships,
our characteristic way of behaving, and our basic beliefs
about life.   They are consistent over time and allow others to
know who we are and relate to us in predictable ways.   This is
the function of identity.   I know who you are, you know who I
am, and we relate to each other on this basis.

Learning and Adaptation

Throughout this discussion on identity I have made
repeated references to the importance of early learning.   I
have not said, however, very much about the process of
learning that forms identity. Basically, learning occurs
through three different but related kinds of processes:
association, imitation and reinforcement.

Effectiveness in life is dependent on our abilities as
learners and the ways we are able to translate learning into
adaptive problem solving.   Our learning and coping style,
again, reflects our basic personality. Many difficulties in
life are a result of failure to acquire (learn) the proper
social and interpersonal skills.   Recovery means unlearning
old habits of thought, behavior, and relating. Recovery means
learning new skills that will allow for more effective living
and eliminate the need for chemical props. The process of
changing old, deeply ingrained habits is not an easy one.

The learning process is like all other human activities, very complicated and always involves the total person. Some learning is social, some takes place in the nervous and muscular system, and some takes place in highly abstract thought processes. Learning involves repetition and reinforcement. The varieties of learning are dependent upon the situation and skills required. In the case of association, it is the process of conditioning that forms the basis of the learning experience. For example, a classic experiment in psychology is the dog and bell. One stimulus is paired with another and the two become associated. In this case, a bell was rung and food was given to a dog. After several repetitions the dog salivated when he heard the bell.

At the human level, if you had a bad accident on the freeway you may experience fear when you get in the car, or get on the freeway, or pass that particular spot. The fear has become associated with a class of stimuli that relate to the accident. A child gets bitten by a dog, the child cries whenever approached by a dog; this is a conditioned response. This is a simple form of learning that does not require intention, thought, effort, or reinforcement.

Some forms of alcohol treatment are based on this form of learning. It is commonly called counter—conditioning or aversive—conditioning. The theory is that if a painful (aversive stimulus) is paired with drinking it will cause the person to develop an aversion to drinking.

In other words, pairing an electric shock or causing the person to become violently ill with drinking or other chemicals will decrease the craving and/or drinking behavior. For some individuals, this form of treatment may be quite effective. For others, they continue despite the painful consequences.

Conditioning is also involved in the acquisition of chemical dependency. The nervous system is easily conditioned when a person experiences pleasure when psycho-active chemicals are used. Chemicals become simultaneously associated with relief from pain or tension and increase of pleasure. This forms the basis for a powerful habit. Other learning is also involved in the acquisition of chemical dependence. A basic law of learning states that if behavior is followed by pleasure or reinforcement, it is more likely to be repeated again. If the behavior is not rewarded or causes pain, it is not likely to be repeated. This is the law of effect. In other words, behavior followed by rewards is learned and eventually will become a habit.

Behavior which is learned this way and then is reinforced intermittently is very hard to change and is most resistant to extinction. Examples of this occur in gambling, abusive relationships, and other forms of addictive behavior. These destructive behaviors are not always followed by pain. We put our money in and nothing happens, then we put our money in and "jackpot!." It is the randomness of the reinforcement that seems to hook us. Getting the jackpot, even though we pay a very high price for it, maintains many destructive habits.

Another form of learning is involved in the acquisition of social behavior. Modeling or imitative learning, occurs just

94

by being in the presence of another person. Imitation tends to be more powerful if the model is warm, accepting, and behaves in a positive—non—aggressive manner. Again, this kind of learning is seen in the destructive legacy of the dysfunctional alcoholic and drug abusing families. Children of these families experience hostility, isolation, lack of affection, inconsistent values, chaotic relationships, lack of discipline and physical and emotional abuse. Substance abuse is modeled as a form of interpersonal problem solving and coping. This is the reality that is modeled, reinforced and conditioned on a daily basis. The literature on Adult Children of Alcoholics is full of information on what is learned in these kinds of families. Basically, children learn (1) to not feel, (2) to not trust, (3) to be overly responsible, and (4) to have high needs for control. It requires very powerful forms of intervention to unlearn and overcome years of abuse, neglect and trauma.

Identity: Development and Crisis

Attachment, thinking, feeling, and learning form the foundation of identity. What is most characteristic of these as a whole is their interdependence as active, dynamic factors in the developmental process of becoming an adult. Growth, transformation and learning—this is the process that makes us uniquely human. Each stage in the developmental process presents unique problems to be solved, tasks to be accomplished, and rewards for passing through to the next stage. Some of these developmental stages are biologically driven; like walking, talking, thinking, puberty, and senescence. Others are socially and psychologically given; like going to school, dating, graduating from school, leaving home, starting a career, marriage, and retirement. These markers are all a part of the "rites of passage" that are a part of human development. With each stage of development there exists the opportunity for growth and crisis. The final goal of development would appear to be a fully functioning adult. And what is that? There are, of course, many definitions. I prefer a very simple one proposed by Freud. He said that being an adult was being able to work and to love. I would add play to the definition.

We begin our identity journey totally dependent on others where our sense of self is given. Who we are is determined by the fact that I am the "Reece Kid", Amos and Viola's boy who lived in the 2 bedroom house on the corner in a small farming town in Washington. Part of these givens are also being Caucasian and male. Gradually, identity becomes more a function of acquired experience. As we go to school and church and interact with others through sports and neighborhood play, an emerging style develops and becomes increasingly unique.

People can distinguish us from our peers because of certain characteristics. Adolescence further shapes this process of becoming. And finally, the struggle for independence reaches its culmination in leaving home and going off to college or work. These profound changes and tasks result in choices that further shape the identity journey. Choosing a spouse, career, school, having children, all of these become part of the adult package. A package which is still evolving as we continue our journey.

All of this growing up takes place through a dynamic interaction between the growing, developing person who is seeking to meet basic physical and psychological needs in a complex social environment. The development of a sense of competence, significance, and meaning is acquired through learning. Whether we develop adequate coping skills is in many ways a function of the skills of our teachers. If we reach adulthood and find ourselves lacking the necessary skills to achieve fulfillment in working, loving, and playing, we may face a crisis of identity. In order to resolve this crisis we must become both teacher and student at the same time. We are on our own now. What becomes of us is up to us now, as adults our identity must come from us. We become the architect, builder, and shaper of our very own selves.

Finally, it is at this time of identity crisis that your sense of self is most at risk. The danger is in the development of an identity of an addict. The cost to self—image is considerable both in terms of how an addict sees him/her self and how others view him/her. The basic truth of addiction is that it takes over and ones' whole life revolves around the lifestyle of being addicted. The identity formulation is — I **am an addict**. This is one's identity. All of the attendant problems go with this. Most of them are associated with loss. Loss of self—esteem, job, family, friends, status, respect and eventually health and life. It takes considerable effort to change this formulation and reverse the losses. A new lifestyle is mandated. One still based on the formulation **I am an addict,** but the word recovery is added. This is the road back to regaining an identity that will lead to recovery of self—respect.

In the following exercises, the goal is to help you explore the basic concepts that were just discussed. The task now is to help you take the ideas and relate them to your personal experience at a feeling level. Through the awareness that you are gaining we are building the foundation for behavior change. By learning to relate to your feelings and history in a new way, gaining insight into yourself and integrating the old pain, you will feel better about yourself. Perhaps you will gradually learn acceptance and let all of the old stuff go. This is how healing and growth take place. **Awareness, Acceptance, Understanding, and Forgiveness.**

NOTES

CHAPTER 3

WHO AM I?

EXERCISE 1

Take a writing tablet and pen. Sit down in a quiet place with some time to spend getting in touch with yourself. Close your eyes and let your mind and feelings connect. Think about who you are. How did you become who you are now? Now, after a few moments start with your present sense of who you are. Write out a few sentences beginning with **I am** _____. And then just fill in the blanks with whatever comes to mind, no matter what. Don't censor it.

EXERCISE 2

Write out more sentences that begin **Others see me as a** _____.

CHAPTER 3

WHO AM I?

EXERCISE 3

Begin sentences with the statement, **My ideal self is**
——————.

EXERCISE 4

Reflect on yourself as a child. What labels did people give you? For example, what names did your parents, peers, and teachers call you? Make a list of these names and labels. How big a part of your identity are these names and labels?

EXERCISE 5

Note significant events, crossroads, traumas and people who significantly changed the course of your life.

EXERCISE 6

Listen to tape #2 "The Inner Journey".

CHAPTER 3

WHO AM I?

Further Reading

Lieberman, Mendel., and Hardie, Marion. Resolving Family and Other Conflicts. Santa Cruz, CA: Unity Press, 1981.

Smith, Manuel J. When I Say No, I Feel Guilty. New York: The Dial Press, 1975.

NOTES

CHAPTER 4 SELF-ESTEEM

> As we are now beginning to understand, man became man in a total celebration of himself, in urges to distinctive self-expression. Unlike the baboon who gluts himself only on food, man nourishes himself mostly on self-esteem.
> Ernest Becker

In the previous chapter, we looked at the origin of identity. In this section we will explore the relationship between self—esteem and addiction. We will see that self—esteem is a crucial part of identity that comes from within and reflects deeply held feelings and attitudes. In other words, self—esteem is the kind of relationship one has with oneself. It's relationship to addiction stems from the fact that low self—esteem comes from deficiency, a feeling of emptiness that leads to a compulsive need to latch onto something external which will provide, often temporarily, a sense of competence, significance and fulfillment. The quest to fill the inner emptiness may become tinged with anxiety and lead to desperate, repetitive, habitual behaviors which are the leading factors in addiction.

In this sense, psychological addiction is an attachment to something or someone outside yourself that you have developed to fill the void. Frequently, people substitute a preoccupation with things, substances, food, work, or sexual activity for healthy human relationships. These activities are substitutes for that which leads to feelings of power, control, significance and meaning. And as such, they give only temporary satisfaction; they don't lead to an inner feeling of self—esteem. I once had a client who said to me, "have you ever been hungry for something and you didn't know what it was? I've tried drugs, alcohol, sex and food and I still have this hunger!" This is an example of what I am writing about, the hunger for self—esteem which often leads to addiction when it is not authentically fulfilled.

If low self—esteem leads to addiction, then it stands to reason that working on the real problem is a necessary and healthy antidote. Building healthy self—esteem means developing confidence and strength from within, in essence, of learning to have control over things which directly affect self—esteem. By gaining a feeling of being O.K. within yourself, the basis of self—esteem is no longer external. As such, it is more stable and enduring over time. Finally, it means cultivating a respectful, compassionate, accepting and intimate friendship with yourself. Often, it is difficult to know which comes first, addiction and then low self—esteem or vice versa. Not everyone with low self—esteem becomes an addict. Let us say, then, that low self—esteem, along with several other factors we have already discussed, play a significant role in creating a vulnerability to addiction. And we may say, with a high degree of certainty, that an eventual casualty of addiction is loss of self—esteem. So let us examine some of the ways that self—esteem is involved and how to restore it.

Essentially, restoration of self—esteem is at the core of the recovery process. And it too involves healing old wounds, learning to take responsibility for the present and setting goals which will ensure a stable sustainable future: one that will provide the necessary conditions for healthy self—esteem.

Understanding self—esteem is important because it is one of the most reliable predictors of a person's mental health. The way that we live is an accurate reflection of our level of self—esteem. For example, a person with low self—esteem tends to devalue himself, has low expectations of achievement and success, feels little control over his life and generally feels inferior to others. A sense of helplessness is often a result of feeling a lack of control and may lead to self—destructive relationships. Self—criticism with guilt, shame, and self—criticism also accompany this problem. A person with high self—esteem, on the other hand, tends to have positive expectations of success, will have warm and non-defensive relationships and is generally much more self—accepting. Along with healthy self—acceptance is a sense of mastery and competence which carries through most situations. Because of the importance of this concept, we will be looking at how it originates as well as how it may be improved.

To comprehend self—esteem we have to do away with the popular misconception that self—esteem is something you have and always have had; that it is something you are born with, and that there is nothing that can be done about it. This idea tends to create a fatalistic view which leads people to believe they have nothing to do with their self—esteem.

Though self-esteem is a rather enduring and consistent aspect of the self, I believe that it is changeable and through awareness and hard work may be changed.

And finally, self-esteem is full of forces which are often in conflict, forces which represent diverse needs, all striving for fulfillment at the same time. Most of this is going on outside our consciousness. Human personality, rather than being like a block of granite or a lump of clay (I can't help it, that's just the way I am) is much more vital. So with this model in mind, let us look at some of the dynamics of self-esteem.

In my clinical experience over the past twenty years, I have found four critical areas related to self-esteem. The first area involves *Competence.* It seems to me that a basic motivating force is the need to master not only our physical environment, but also the complexities of the social and psychological world. Whether it is in play, school, sports, business or relationships, people seem to strive to master the task at hand. Usually, when we feel competent, our self-esteem is high and vice versa. Feelings of depression, helplessness, and incompetence are usually correlated with low self-esteem. Power is a close cousin to competence. Power has a somewhat negative connotation for many people. Probably because they have been victimized by the abuse of power.

It might be well for you to take a moment here to reflect on your own feelings of power and competence. Think of how failure to achieve competence makes you feel. Focus on your feelings of power in relationship to other people.

When the demands of adaptation are met, then high
self—esteem usually results, which is to say, one feels
competent and has received positive reinforcement from others
for mastery of important stages. The opposite is also true,
particularly if the conditions persist over a long period of
time. Feelings of inadequacy, helplessness, inferiority and
low self—esteem are closely associated with depression and low
control. Self—esteem, competence, and power are inter—related.
If one has achieved a sense of competence and mastery, then
usually self—esteem is a by—product of this accomplishment.
The opposite is also true. The person who feels incompetent,
inadequate, or inferior usually also feels helpless,
ineffectual, and low in self— esteem. This is particularly
true if these conditions have persisted over a long period of
time. It is very damaging to self—esteem to continually
strive for mastery and success and to receive little
reinforcement from others or to not receive the expected
reward for effort. Effort without reward leads to reduced
motivation and eventually the person gives up; learned
helplessness is the result.

A second necessary condition for healthy self—esteem is
psychological independence: *Individuation.* The thrust of
human development is from dependence to independence. Born in
a state of total dependence on caretakers, the infant evolves
through many important stages to achieve autonomy of
functioning. If development is normal, and social conditions
are optimum, the infant grows up to be capable of self—
actualization. As we all know, however, conditions are seldom

107

perfect and we grow up impaired to one degree or another. Infancy is a time of great vulnerability. The newborn is dependent on everyone for safety, security, and basic physical needs as well as psychological nurturance and guidance. Without good caretaking, the infant either dies or becomes developmentally impaired. In adulthood, we should be able to provide those functions for ourselves which were initially provided by caretakers. This is one measure of healthy self-esteem and psychological maturity.

Psychological independence, as many people think, does not mean never needing anyone. Often the person who takes the stance of not needing anyone is frightened of his/her own unmet dependency needs, needs which everyone has. It is the ability to deal with the needs of others, as well as one's own, which is the mark of emotional maturity. The dependence/independence conflict creates a very powerful undercurrent in many relationships. An undercurrent which often breeds hostility, resentment, and fear. This topic has received a great deal of attention in recent years and is usually discussed as *Co-dependency.*

The fearful, needy, dependent person who needs love in order to feel worthwhile and is unable to function without attachment to another, soon becomes an emotional burden to the partner. Clinging, jealousy, and feeling empty are signals of emotional dependency. The emotionally dependent person often feels powerless over their sources of love and self-esteem: powerless, because it is not possible to control the world of others sufficiently to fill the inner void created by the absence of self—esteem. As a defense against these feelings of powerlessness and neediness, which can leave one feeling infantile and vulnerable, some people react in the totally opposite direction by being "super—independent." By not needing anyone, or letting anyone get close, the individual presents a mask of strength and competence. In reality, this person may not be able to experience true intimacy because of the feared trap of dependency. Independence means choice, responsibility, and freedom.   It means taking the responsibility for what happens and not blaming life or others. "Look what you did to me", is the classic position of the dependent person who blames others. "If it weren't for you is the dependent persons alibi. The independent person does not blame. Independence means creating through daily choices the kind of person one is becoming. In this sense, we are the author of our own poem. We are the writer, director, and producer of our own melodrama. As one of my clients put it, "I feel like I get up and create myself every day." Paradoxically, when we fail to exercise our freedom with responsibility we end up in positions of total dependence where other's run our lives. Hospitals and prisons are full of such people who have failed to achieve true independence.

Life lived independently is not lived apart from people. For this reason, relationships are crucial to self—esteem. This is the third dimension of self—esteem: *Interdependence,* which gets worked out in the dynamic tension of intimacy vs. isolation. For some individuals, relationships have been so accompanied by trauma, pain, disillusionment, and abuse that they have retreated into a world of isolation. This position is characterized by the motto "don't let anyone get to you." This defense keeps people at a safe distance; it also creates tremendous loneliness. Isolated people are vulnerable to stress, anxiety, and depression. They have higher rates of illness, suicide, and drug use. Though an addict has tremendous needs to feel loved and significant, the great paradox is that addiction leads to being alone and eventually driving everyone away. The only thing left to depend on is the chemical of choice.

Relationships provide emotional support and comfort in time of need. The dilemma of being human is the need for relationships in which to express our full humanity. For it is in loving and being loved that we reach our greatest fulfillment as human beings. While relationships fulfill our greatest needs, they also evoke our greatest fears. Abandonment, rejection, humiliation, exploitation; these are the feared and painful possibilities of being in an intimate relationship. This is the ambivalence of relationships—fear and need, love and hate. The capacity for intimacy means being able to love in spite of vulnerability and the possibilities of abandonment, rejection, and injury. The capacity for intimacy is measured by the ability to tolerate anger and hurt without resorting to isolation as a defense. Intimacy is being known through emotional contact and closeness with another in which the deepest and most inner parts of the self are exposed without defenses. Everyone has the secret inner world, the inner sanctum, I call it.

Intimacy is being able to allow another into this sacred place. Intimacy also means being able to be in another's secret, inner world without injuring the other person. We have all, no doubt, experienced the pain, hurt, and anger when another failed to respect or appreciate us in our inner most self. The self is most exposed when we love. In order to be capable of true intimacy as experienced in interdependence, we must be capable of being alone as well as unafraid of being dependent.

Finally, self—esteem is based on a sense of significance and meaning. Victor Frankl, a famous philosopher and psychiatrist has written that the need for meaning is essential for being human. He wrote this after he was imprisoned in a Nazi concentration camp and lost his family to the Holocaust. He argues that it is only through being able to make sense out of what happens to us, are we able to endure. Lack of meaning and significance can lead to feelings of hopelessness and despair. With no sense of purpose, a person often feels aimless and useless. Those who have lost their purpose and direction suffer from Anomie. This is a condition of despair which often leads to suicide. When the inner world collapses from meaninglessness, people often feel there is no longer any reason to go on. Those who experience Anomie (meaninglessness) often feel like outsiders, lone wolves, who wander about on the outside of society. The person suffering from Anomie is alienated from society, feels no sense of belonging, and does not reap the benefit of being able to participate in any of the rituals, ceremonies, and

111

symbols of a society which provides a sense of purpose, meaning, values and community. Commonly held values and shared experience bind the human community together. Finding a place within the community, by belonging, and feeling affirmed are central to a basic sense of self—esteem and esteem from others.

Independence, intimacy, competence, significance, and meaning are characteristic of a person with high self—esteem and the sign of a well lived life. Conversely, dependency, isolation, helplessness, and meaninglessness are reflections of low—self—esteem. Low self—esteem typifies the life of "quiet desperation and despair". The dynamics of self—esteem involve the quest to preserve and enhance one's self through daily transactions in the marketplace of life.

In brief, in our discussion on self—esteem, we have seen that it is a dynamic process of interaction in which the individual is engaged in a continuous dialogue with a complex environment. At stake in all of these transactions is **Self—Esteem.** While the individual is struggling to adapt, cope, accommodate, and maintain balance and security, he/she is also attempting the Self—Project: a project which involves preserving and enhancing self—esteem. Maintaining self—esteem usually involves trying to meet one's needs for intimacy, independence, competence, and significance, while coming to terms with the demands of reality. As we are all aware, this is no easy task, but it is what is required of us all.

Furthermore, we have discussed the important task of building a stable and secure world of relationships where the person feels valued, cared for, and cherished. This enduring world of significance is vulnerable to crisis if factors or circumstances occur which threaten to overwhelm a person's coping defenses. Crises of self—esteem and identity may also occur if a person is unable to maintain a meaningful view of himself or his world. For example, victims of major air disasters have their view of personal invulnerability destroyed. Accidents are things which happen to others. Losing someone in an air crash overwhelms the defenses, violates the personal view of the self and also violates the schema of a just and stable world. When confronted with this kind of a tragedy, a person is confronted with a major stressor which threatens the person's whole self—system. Threats also may occur from the gradual build up of stress over time which leaves the individual vulnerable and low on coping resources. In any case, when people feel victimized or experiences a major threat to self—esteem, they are likely to feel helpless, needy, weak, vulnerable, inadequate and overwhelmed.

The extent of the crisis depends on the strength of the person's coping defenses, the nature of the stressor, and finally the quality of the recovery environment in which the person exists. These factors have important implications for our understanding of the recovery process.

Finally, we have seen that crises, when handled properly, may lead to new levels of self—esteem, new levels of relationships with others, a greater sense of significance, and an over all growth in the ability of the person to function more independently. Healing takes place as we accept responsibility for our own self-esteem and courageously pursue the quest for authentic identity.

In order to heal, to begin the restoration of self-esteem, we must deal with some of the old wounds which are perhaps contributing to the problem. As was discussed in the previous chapter, we all have histories that have contributed to our pain and present dilemma, and had a negative impact on our self-esteem.

Sources of Low Self-Esteem

What are some of the sources of low self-esteem? Usually, low self-esteem is traceable to the early, formative years in which the child is most dependent, vulnerable, and naive. Early interactions with parents set the tone for development of attitudes toward the self. Essentially, we relate to ourselves and treat others the way our parents treated us.

Some of the more damaging experiences can be parents who are overly critical, harsh and demanding and who fail to nurture with warmth and acceptance. The residual of this kind of parenting is the most common source of low self-esteem: perfectionism. Perfectionism leads to chronic feelings of inferiority. Perfectionists rarely get to feel good about themselves because performance is rarely good enough. Self-esteem is based on **doing** rather than **being**.

A second critical factor in low self-esteem is the experience of early childhood trauma and loss. Divorce, death of a parent, abandonment, early childhood illness, and other disruptions may create long term anxiety about dependency.

This contributes to the inner void; that ancient love hunger which leads to over—dependency on people, chemicals, or whatever masks this emptiness.

A third common cause of low self—esteem is parental abuse. Abuse may come in many forms; physical, sexual, or emotional. This may, depending of course; on severity, lead to insecurity, lack of trust, difficulty in intimacy, guilt, rage, shame, and the inability to freely love and be loved. The legacy of abuse is enormous. Adults abused as children may become perpetual victims or victimizers. They are usually hostile, suspicious and ambivalent in relationships. A very common problem is a deep seated rage which is turned against the self and is experienced as self—loathing, disgust and inadequacy. Understandably, these individuals are very prone to addiction and other forms of self destructive behaviors.

Finally, parental alcoholism and drug abuse is a major contributor to problems with self—esteem. Chronic parental substance abuse creates a chaotic, unreliable family atmosphere in which it is difficult to develop a basic sense of trust, security, or self—esteem. The literature on A.C.A.'s (Adult Children of Alcoholics) is filled with information describing its effects on children.

The denial, poor communication, and outright insanity often lead to a sense of unreality and a feeling that chaos is normal. It is generally accepted that many adult children of alcoholics grow up with personality characteristics such as (1) preoccupation with control, (2) avoidance of feelings, (3) difficulty trusting others, (4) being overly responsible, (5)

black and white thinking, (6) over-compliance, or an excessive
eagerness to please, (7) difficulties in trusting their
perception of reality, and (8) low self esteem. This cluster
of characteristics is often manifested as a deep seated sense
of insecurity which creates anxiety and depression. Drugs and
alcohol are frequently used as a form of self-prescribed
medication.

From this discussion we may conclude that the sources of
low self-esteem are complex, traumatic and often the result of
life-long experiences which may result in considerable pain.
This relationship between pain and self-esteem often results
in addiction. We have been exploring this relationship in the
preceding pages. Now let us turn our discussion to looking at
the pathways to self-esteem. Again, we are concerned with
recovery and healing, and in this instance we want to discover
ways in which self-esteem may be regained.

In my view, healing self-esteem involves healing old
wounds, learning to have a new and healthy relationship with
ourselves, and building a new way of living which will meet
our needs for competency, significance, and meaning.

Since this whole program is concerned with these areas,
we will discuss them in their entirety in subsequent, separate
chapters to delve into each area in greater depth. In sum,
healthy self-esteem comes from within and involves a loving,
friendly, intimate, compassionate, respectful relationship
with ourselves. It also is about being able to meet our needs
for love, security, and competence through meaningful
connections with others. Mastery over that which involves our

self-esteem will break the link with addiction. If we are addicted, it will be only to feeling good about ourselves and doing those things which foster self-love.

NOTES

SELF—ESTEEM

EXERCISE 1

1. To get a feel for your own level of self—esteem, rate yourself on the degree to which you trust, accept and have confidence in yourself.

```
0    1    2    3    4    5    6    7    8    9    10
<very low self—esteem            >very high self—esteem
```

Self esteem is largely dependent on recognizing and meeting basic human needs.

Read the following list and make a check next to the needs which are currently being met.

CHAPTER 4

SELF-ESTEEM

EXERCISE 2

BASIC HUMAN NEEDS

1. Physical safety and security.   _____

2. Physical Health— including exercise, diet, and
   healthful habits.   _____

3. Financial Security.   _____

4. Friendship—support, respect and attention from
   others; loyalty and trust.   _____

5. Significance— being validated, respected and
   listened to.   _____

6. Able to feel, express and share feelings.   _____

7. A sense of belonging and community.   _____

8. Nurturing and love.   _____

9. Sexual—being touched and touching.   _____

10. Intimacy—opportunity to disclose inner feelings
    and reveal self.   _____

11. Competence— A sense of accomplishment and
    progress toward goals.   _____

12. Feeling fulfilled in some area of importance
    to you.   _____

13. Freedom and independence.   _____

14. Creativity.   _____

15. Fun and play.   _____

16. Spiritual awareness and expression.   _____

Look at the list and note which needs aren't being met.

CHAPTER 4

SELF—ESTEEM

EXERCISE 3

NEED MEETING GOALS

Categorize your needs into areas. They usually fall into 5 areas (1) Physical (2) Safety (3) relationship (4) Competence (5) Self—actualizing.

Target one need in each area to work on in the next month.

Make a systematic plan for how you plan to meet that goal.

Make a list of your most important personal goals.

— For the next month

— For the next 6 months

— For the next year

— For the next 5 years

What obstacles might you encounter in meeting your goals?

What keeps you from doing what you want?

CHAPTER 4

SELF—ESTEEM

EXERCISE 4

LIST OF PERSONAL ACCOMPLISHMENTS

When we are not feeling good about ourselves we often look at what we haven't accomplished. Make a list of all that you have accomplished.

School

Work and Career

Home and Family

Athletics

Community

Creativity—Arts—Hobbies

Awards

Personal Growth

Others

Crises Weathered

Life Lessons Learned

CHAPTER 4

SELF—ESTEEM

Further Reading

Mangini,Shirley. Secrets of Self—Esteem. Canoga Park, Ca.: N.O.V.A. 1985.

McKay, Mathew, and Fanning, Patrick. Self—Esteem. Oakland, Ca.: New Harbinger Pub. 1987.

Whitfield, Charles. Healing the Child Within. Pompano Beach, Fl.: Health Communications. 1987.

Woititz, Janet. Adult Children of Alcoholics. Hollywood, Fl.: Heath Communications. 1983.

CHAPTER 5

THINKING-FEELING-BEHAVING

> Your habitual way of explaining bad events, your
> explanatory style, is more than just the words you mouth when
> you fail. It is a habit of thought, learned in childhood and
> adolescence. Your explanatory style stems directly from your
> view of your place in the world--whether you think you are
> valuable and deserving, or worthless and hopeless.
> Martin Seligman, Ph.D.

The phone rang and I answered it. The call was from my supervisor's secretary. He wanted to see me in his office as soon as possible. I began immediately to worry. I thought about my work over the past few weeks. What have I done wrong? I must be in big trouble because he wants to see me right away. My heart began to pound, I had that awful sinking feeling in my stomach, I began to think about what I would do if I was fired, I saw my future going down the drain. When I got to his office that afternoon, my palms were sweaty, my knees felt weak, and my pulse was rapid. He invited me into his office. Then he informed me that a staff psychologist had left and they wanted to change my position from intern to staff level.

This example illustrates the complex relationship between stimulus, perception, beliefs, self-talk, feeling and behavior. The *stimulus*-boss wants to see you. The *perception*-I am in trouble. The *belief*-the only time an authority figure notices me is to criticize me because I never do anything right. *Self-talk*—I wonder where I screwed up this time, I am in trouble, I am going to be fired, nothing good ever happens to me. It's the end of the world. *Behavior*—worry, anxiety and self criticism. The things we believe, and the things we tell ourselves for most people are an automatic, habitual mental activity that profoundly influences behavior and feelings. Most people take for granted their thinking and feeling and don't realize how it may effect the outcome of their lives and seldom understand that it is something they are doing to themselves.

My response in this example reveals what I believed about myself, my competence and authority figures. Essentially, the stimulus of the phone call is a neutral event. How I responded to it was a function of acquired (learned) experience. There are a number of possible ways that I could have responded differently. How I responded was based on my interpretation of the event and the subsequent things I told myself. Let us examine the relationship between beliefs and our self—talk in order to understand how we make ourselves anxious and upset. The fact is, it's what we say to ourselves in response to events that mainly determines our mood and feelings. What we say to ourselves in large measure is a function of our fundamental—deeply held beliefs about ourselves, others, the nature of the world, and our place in it. What is crucial here is that we are not born with these predispositions to think catastrophically, fearfully, and self—critically. They are learned, and therefore can be unlearned.

In the sections on identity and self—esteem we learned that cognitive development resulted in the organization of experience into *schemata—mental maps*. These habitual mental representations are beliefs about the world and become the basis for the attributions (explanations) we make about cause and effect.

In the example I am using from my own experience we see clearly how this works. The self—schema, I am no good, interacted with the father schema, the demeaning, critical father whom I couldn't please. The obvious result is to feel anxious whenever the boss—dad wants to see me. In my early experience, when dad wanted to see me, it was because we were going to the woodshed with his barber's razor strap. Again, a considerable cause for alarm.

What is most evident about these schemata—beliefs is that they are automatic, they function for the most part unconsciously, we accept them as true, and they serve as self—fulfilling prophecies.

These beliefs serve many important functions. In fact, we could not live in society without them. Their first function is to organize experience in ways that make it intelligible and meaningful.

A second major function is to make us a member of society. Societies are organized by means of adopting shared beliefs, values and myths that explain the universe, our place in it, and spell out the rules which govern behavior. People who violate the rules and do not conform to dominant social mores are labeled deviants. Beliefs and meaning systems also serve to make behavior stable and consistent over time. Imagine what it would be like to wake up each day and look in the mirror and not know who you are and not know what is expected of you, as well.

Finally, beliefs are formed into an organized system which provides basic assumptions about life. These assumptions provide explanations about why things happen. For example, Don Drysdale, a former pitcher for the Los Angeles Dodgers and Roy Campenella, a former catcher for the Dodgers died within a short period of time. Tom Lasorda, the Dodger manager explained their deaths by saying "I guess God needed a pitcher and catcher in heaven." Each of us tries to answer why things happen to us on the basis of a set of assumptions about life that we have learned from our parents, teachers, and institutions. Some of these beliefs are helpful, some are not. We all have our own private collection.

Let us look at some of these " beliefs"

(1) Gender related beliefs. For example, boy's don't cry, women are weak.

(2) If too many good things happen you'd better start worrying.

(3) It's better to not try than risk failure and disappointment.

(4) We are all victims of fate.

(5) Don't expect anything and you will never be disappointed.

(6) I am powerless to make anything good happen for me.

(7) I can control life by worrying.

(8) Better to be safe than sorry.

(9)   Life is too hard and dangerous for me, I need others to take care of me.

(10) My feelings don't matter.

These beliefs are commonly held by many people. Take a look at them and see how these beliefs would affect feelings and behavior. Are they helpful? Why not? What's wrong with them? What kind of behavior would they lead to?

It is sometimes difficult to recognize our own beliefs and faulty assumptions because we take them for granted. The first step in changing our dysfunctional beliefs is to begin to question them and catch yourself in the act of thinking and acting on them. One of the ways to begin working with this problem is to take a look at some of the beliefs you have perhaps already uncovered about yourself in the section on self—esteem. Take an idea you have about yourself and ask yourself the following questions:

(1)   What is the belief based on? Is there any evidence for it being true based on your life experience. For example, take the statement "I can't do anything right, I'm a failure." What is the evidence that this is true?

(2)   Is the belief always true?

(3)   Does this belief take in the whole picture? Some beliefs serve to screen out any contrary evidence. Does it take in both the positive and the negative?

(4)   What purpose does this belief serve your self—esteem? Does it reinforce negative and depressive thoughts or does it allow you to feel good about yourself.

(5)   Where did the belief come from? Is it yours or did others impose it on you?

127

It is often helpful to examine beliefs in order to understand their origin and function. While these beliefs may have served an important purpose when they originated, they may not be useful now. For example, my father ridiculed me for crying as a child. As an adult I have often found it difficult to cry when sad or when I experience a loss.

Since most of our core beliefs and basic assumptions evolved and became fixed in childhood, let us look at some of these childhood assumptions which may still influence our actions, feelings, and beliefs now. For simplicity of description I have organized these beliefs into types of children, because that's when they were acquired. Obviously we may have many of these qualities, but they do help us in our understanding to stereotype them.

For purposes of our discussion, think of how you came to see the world. What your parents taught you and what your early experiences with peers and other significant others were. Try to remember how you felt as a needy, dependent, helpless, naive child. This dimension of ourselves is often referred to as the "inner child". What type of inner child do you have? By learning about this part of yourself, you may come to understand some of the ways your beliefs about yourself, others, and the world were formed.

I have categorized these into six basic types:

1. the shamed child
2. the frightened child
3. the spoiled child
4. the guilty child

5.   the abused child

6.   the loved child.

Each of these types of children view the world differently and consequently experiences it differently.

The **shamed child** is one whose parents ridiculed and demeaned him/her for existing. This child comes to feel "I am fundamentally flawed". The shamed child feels embarrassed and disappointed for being inadequate. Low self—esteem is the hallmark of shame. The residue of shame is a sense of not being lovable and that success in life is not possible or deserved. Others are seen as more powerful. The shamed child is not good at pursuing his/her own needs. It seems in this belief system that everyone else is more important. Shame leads to tremendous feelings of emptiness and isolation. The shamed child sees the world as the shaming parent: hostile, unrewarding, and un—nurturing. The shamed child often grows up isolated and alone with no close personal attachments; helplessness and depression are the result.

The **frightened child** obviously feels that the world is a very threatening place. Looking at the world from this perspective, the frightened child is afraid to take risks, everything is a potential catastrophe. The frightened child is preoccupied with what if.... Fear often keeps the person who experiences the world this way paralyzed by inaction. Just as the parents were no doubt fearful and overprotective, the adult, seeing the world as a fearful child needs a great deal of reassurance and support. The fearful child is often sensitive and prone to worry. Anxiety is the dominant feeling, even over small signs of trouble. The fearful child is often shy, insecure and reluctant to participate in the rough and tumble of childhood play.

The **spoiled child** is one whose parents over indulged him/her to the point that he/she has come to expect the world to give special attention. Often demanding and easily injured when others don't recognize his/her greatness, he/she pouts when frustrated. Giving is difficult and appropriate rules and boundaries have not been learned. The spoiled child treats others as objects. The spoiled child is obviously very immature and self—preoccupied as an adult. The world of others is seen as existing merely as an extension of the spoiled child's world of wants and needs. This person may appear to have high self-esteem, but it is not based on love of self, but rather on props related to attention, adulation and external signs of status.

The **guilty child** is driven by never feeling good enough. This child lives with constant criticism and unduly high expectations. Little reward is given for achievement, and failure is always pointed out. As an adult you criticize yourself relentlessly for imagined flaws and ignore any positive qualities. Self—esteem is based on being perfect. Quite often the voice of criticism in the head is personified by a critical parent. Labels and name calling are the favorite mode of self—talk. The guilty child is often critical of others as well. No one measures up in this system. As you can see, the perfectionist is often chronically stressed, constricted and joyless. Perfectionists rarely play, let their hair down, get messy, or engage in any spontaneous activity.

The *abused child* is characterized by anger and ambivalence in approach to the world. Often the abused child assumes the role of a victim. Feelings of helplessness and hopelessness predominate. Depression alternating with anger is a natural response to the abuse experienced at the hands of violent and unloving parents. Relationships are ambivalent because abused children have had their trust shattered. As a result, abused children as adults find themselves caught between need and fear. Relationships, because of fear and anger, are volatile and unstable. The world is seen as a projection of the abusing parent. Self—destructive behavior and patterns of victimization are the legacy of abused children who have become adults. The abused—victim-child believes that nothing will change and life is hopeless. Learned helplessness is expressed as an "I can't", or "it won't do any good to try." In essence, "I don't matter and nothing I do matters."

The *loved child,* in contrast to all of these other children, is most fortunate indeed. This child is raised in a stable, caring and nurturing environment. The parents respect and nurture the child's growing individuality. Competence and success are praised and failures are met with understanding, compassion and encouragement. Self—esteem is high because the loved child loves him/herself in the way that the parents loved him/her. The world is seen as a place full of possibility and is met with confidence. This child grows up to respect others and is capable of loving because he/she was loved.

Most people I deal with are not able to relate to the loved child. This is seen as an Ozzie and Harriet fantasy. It is true that few of us were fully loved enough to have experienced this ideal state. However, the important aspect is whether or not we got enough love to promote self-esteem and foster the ability to be a loving adult.

Perhaps as you look at each of these child types you saw something of yourself in each. Take some time to think about each and see which of them you most strongly identify with. See how viewing the world through a child's eyes plays a role in your thinking, feeling, and behaving. You may want to rate each profile on the degree to which you feel it is like you. Rate it from one to six. One being least like you and six being most like you.

Now that you have perhaps identified some of the early beliefs and characteristic ways of approaching the world and seeing yourself, let us turn our attention to the topic of self-talk as an outgrowth of beliefs from our inner child.

Throughout our discussion I have repeatedly emphasized the importance of perception as being responsible for determining how we will respond to a given situation. As part of this discussion I have also underscored the importance of *inner dialogue.* Few people realize the relationship between what we tell ourselves about something and how we feel. This is the subconscious and automatic quality of our thinking. In fact, most people in response to a situation often say "He made me feel guilty." When I attempt to counter this argument with the suggestion that quite to the contrary, He didn't make you feel guilty but rather you made you feel guilty, it is usually met with resistance.

We are accustomed to looking at situations by blaming. Let us use the example I began with to illustrate: phone call, (stimulus) worry, (response) therefore the phone call (he—the boss) created fear in me. Let me suggest an alternate explanation. The phone call is a rather ambiguous stimulus, I could have responded to it in any number of possible ways. I made me feel anxious because I interpreted it as a threat. I did that because of fear of my father. Secondly, I maintained and increased the fear by my anxious thoughts about all of the terrible things that were going to happen to me because I had done something wrong. By looking at the situation in a new way we can interject this alternate perspective. We are responsible for how we feel. It is our expectations based on our previous experience which lead to the fearful self-talk. This is a very important difference, one that is hard to grasp, particularly if we are habituated to think as a victim: "He made me do it!"

It is easier to blame the way you feel on something or someone outside yourself than to take responsibility for your reactions. But in taking ownership of our thoughts, feelings, and behavior we can begin to acquire mastery, competence, and control over our lives. The awareness of this alternative perspective: that we are largely responsible for how we are, is empowering once it is accepted. This simple realization which begins with awareness makes it possible to move into assessing problems and designing action strategies. It can only begin if we own our thoughts, feelings, and behavior.

Self—talk has several important qualities. The first of which is that it is largely habitual and automatic. Secondly, it is acquired. It is based on previous experience. Because of this, we believe it. We always act as if it were true. This is why it is hard to get people to change. For example, a client of mine has had a series of poor relationships with men culminating in a date rape. She tells me with conviction, "all men are scum". In her experience this is true. This illustrates another characteristic of self—talk and beliefs, they are over—generalizations based on a negative experience, which lead to being self-fulfilling prophecies.

Another aspect of self—talk is that it is usually associated with strong feelings. For this reason it feels even more real and is therefore harder to change. " But it really is true," she argues.

Over the past few years a number of therapists have explored these problems and have found that anxious, depressed and traumatized people tend to think in distorted, unrealistic, and illogical ways. These discoveries have led to a form of therapy called cognitive behavior modification. Aaron Beck and David Burns have described these distorted ways of thinking in great detail. I have included a questionnaire from their work in the exercise section which will help you recognize this kind of thinking. They have found that learning to recognize and counter these distorted ways of thinking will be instrumental in helping you view yourself in a more realistic, objective fashion. Once you master this you will feel much more optimistic.

Let's examine some of these distorted ways of thinking and talking to ourselves.

(1) Filtering

This is a way of selectively perceiving an event. If we are depressed, we see only the negative, if we are fearful, we see danger. Filtering also involves memory. Perfectionists only look at failure. People with low self-esteem only see their lack of success. By filtering we respond to only one detail, and then magnify its importance. The end result is that all fears, losses, and irritations become exaggerated to the exclusion of everything else. Key words in filtering are: terrible, awful, horrendous, disgusting, and I can't stand it.

(2) Polarized Thinking

This is also called black and white thinking. Everything is perceived as extremes; there is no middle ground. Things are good or bad, wonderful or horrible. In this extreme world there is little room for the nuances of gray. Because of extreme thinking reactions are also extreme.

(3) Over-Generalization

This distortion stems from making conclusions and founding our beliefs on one experience and then generalizing from it. Usually, the experience is a negative one. You are overgeneralizing when your boss criticizes you and you conclude "I can't do anything right, I'll never be any good at this job." Your conclusions neglect all evidence to the

135

contrary and lead to erroneous conclusions about your ability. It also leads to depression and victimization. Cue words are never, always, none, nobody, and everybody.

(4) Mind Reading

One of the major causes of misunderstanding and poor communication is based on mind reading. This activity involves assuming what other people are thinking based on their behavior. She didn't call because she doesn't like me. The boss called because he wants to yell at me are both examples of mind reading. We mind read through a process called projection, which involves basing our assumptions on our own intuition, feelings, and thoughts and assuming that everyone else is thinking that way. Again, this activity usually occurs in a situation where we do not have accurate information or feedback.

(5) Victimization

Thinking like a victim leads to feeling and acting like a victim. Victimization stems from the belief that you are powerless and that others have more power and control than you do. It also leads to blaming situations and others for problems which may arise. This kind of thinking is a result of distorting your power and control. This can go in one direction that leads to believing you have no control or it can go in the direction of believing you should be able to control everything. When we feel omnipotent we are exaggerating our own power and responsibility. The reality is we are not responsible for the world's happiness or for meeting everyone's needs. Even though we may feel like it.

(6) Hysterical Thinking

"The sky is falling" screamed Chicken Little. We engage in this kind of catastrophic thinking whenever our emotions overtake our reason. This kind of thinking occurs when our emotions become the filter for our reasoning. When we are angry, or sad, depressed, or joyful, the world looks quite different. You make a significant error when you look at the world on the basis of feelings alone. The logic of emotional reasoning is: all the bad things I feel about me and the world must be true because they *feel* true.

(7) The Just World

This is a universal illusion. We all operate on the assumption that the world should be a fair and just place where good is rewarded, evil is punished and people play by the rules. This becomes distorted thinking when we operate from a position of rigid rules and legalistic expectations. Often, people who do this are tyrannized by their own shoulds and oughts and seek to impose them on others. This leads to a great deal of self-criticism, intolerance of mistakes in ourselves and an unreasonable need to be *right* all the time. Should is the key word in this kind of thinking and the lament, "it's not fair," is frequently exclaimed.

These brief examples of distorted thinking are but a few of the ways we make errors in thinking which lead to erroneous feeling and behavior. The thing which needs to be underscored is that *perception is everything.* It is a function of interpretation which is based on our expectations at the time, our beliefs about what just occurred and what we told

137

ourselves about it. Our feelings and subsequent behavior follow our perceptions.

I have discussed these issues in order to bring into awareness this complex process of thinking in order to understand ways we may contribute to our own problems. Let's turn our attention briefly to how to combat distorted thinking and self—talk.

The first step in the process of combating distorted thinking is discovering your *primary mental set,* or as Martin Seligman calls it, *explanatory style.* Each of us has a habitual way of approaching and understanding the world. All of our behavior follows from this. Various psychological theories are based on this. The most notable is Transactional Analysis. Another is Rational—emotive Therapy. They have coined the terms "Life Script and Life—Position or Ego states." Basically, what they are describing is our world view. This is that complex belief system which you developed as a child, through interaction with your parents, and other teachers. Through the process of enculturation you became a member of society. In other words, you adopted the language, beliefs, values, roles, and rules of your culture. Additionally, you were a member of a family which had its own unique window on the world. Through this early training, you came to see and experience the world in a habitual way.

I described several possible positions as world—views based on child ego states. These are (1) **shame,** (2) **fear,** (3) **indulgence** (4) **guilt,** (5) **victim** (6) **love.** Each of these life positions have characteristic ways of thinking, feeling and behaving which are consistent over time and strongly determine our personality. They make us unique.

In order to change, you must learn to recognize and identify which of these ego states best describes your life—script, inner child, mental set, or explanatory style. In the previous chapters I had you explore your personal history and sources of your identity and self—esteem. It's time to draw on that material.

In order to change your distorted thinking you will go through a six stage process. I have found the following steps very helpful in changing thinking.

Step I   Stopping the World

Obviously, we can't literally stop the world, but we can stop our inner world by declaring a time out. In order to do this we must literally catch ourselves in the act. This means interrupting the flow of our habitual experience. If we allow habits to run their course, they have predictable outcomes. This is because habits are automatic behavior. So the first step is to identify your characteristic ego state (life script) and begin to see how it influences all of your life: --Name the Emotion---- . Are you a spoiled child? How does a spoiled child characteristically think, feel and act? So a way to catch yourself in the act is when you are having a temper tantrum to literally tell yourself **STOP!** Then having done this, really see how this behavior works. See yourself in action from a vantage point outside yourself. Look at your tantrum like a videotape. From the perspective of a detached observer record the event. This will lead naturally into the next step.

Step 2 Record

By recording a typical event or situation in which your ego state is dominant, you will gain important information about yourself. Record in detail what happened. Look for triggering stimuli. What events immediately prior to the distress are operative? Get to know these well. Make a list of things which push your button. This alone is going to give you greater awareness and control. Record exactly what you were feeling at the time. Describe the feelings. Have you felt them before? When and under what circumstances do you remember feeling these feelings for the first time? Record any memories that come to mind. This will add to your awareness. As part of this process, it is important to write down any thoughts you had at the moment, these are the things we tell ourselves about what we are doing and why, as well as the behavior of other people. Finally, write down your behavior, what you actually did before, during and after the event. Just describe it, do not judge, label, criticize or evaluate it. Just record it.

Step 3 Identify the Belief

The best indicator of a distorted assumption is the presence of painful emotions. When we feel chronically anxious, depressed, angry, helpless, or disgusted with ourselves, it is because we are acting on painful conclusions

140

that may have been true at the time of learning, but are now no longer helpful. Most people still believe and cherish their rules, however it is now time to question them. See if the result is poor decision making, lowered self—esteem, painful emotions, interpersonal conflict and stress. To uncover a distorted belief ask yourself— "What do I believe to be true about this situation? Once you can identify an assumption you can then see how you act it out.

For example, in the illustration I used to begin this chapter can you identify some of the assumptions I was making at the time? What was the emotion? What was the ego state? I was operating from the position of the shamed child. In that situation, I believed that I would be criticized. Why? Because I believe that I am fundamentally flawed. I also believed that authority figures were out to punish me. Why? Because they are hostile and punitive. Can you see how these beliefs naturally trigger emotions and behavior? When we start with a false premise, everything else that follows is false. Identify a belief by going back to the time when you experienced it as a child. Do you continue to experience it as an adult? Identify what you felt and thought. Do you see how that continues to shape your present behavior?

Step 4 Assess the Belief

Now you are ready to uncover and restructure the beliefs and assumptions which underlie much of your behavior. This is where you must begin to question your own expectations. Just as I in my own therapy came to see how my relationship with my father influenced my beliefs about myself. We assess our beliefs by applying the reality test. Return to the questions I suggested earlier. What is the evidence for this belief? Is the belief always true? Am I engaging in distorted thinking which filters out the positive or ignores the whole picture? Does this belief accurately serve my self—esteem and promote my welfare? Finally, is this my belief or is it a dysfunctional residual from childhood? In other words, in assessing our beliefs we need to see if they are rational; based on reality, are our own, and serve our well—being? Are they functional?

Step 5 Re—cognize

The word recognition as defined by Webster means to perceive clearly. It is an act of knowing. In the context of our discussion, I would like to suggest that we use the term in a dual way. That we begin with seeing our behavior clearly (recognize). And then I would add a second dimension to the term by hyphenating it. Re—Cognize. When we Re—cognize, we are engaging in the act of reframing our beliefs. Reframing situations or our thoughts about it doesn't necessarily change the event, but it changes the meaning for us. If we change what the experience means to us, our responses will change. Some call this redefining or relabeling, but whatever the term, what we are doing is attaching a new response by perceiving it differently. You have the content the same, but put new meaning around it.

For example, we feel a violent push from behind while

standing in line at a theater and feel immediately angry. We turn around and see that a man on crutches has lost his balance and fallen into us. We perceive the event differently because we see his "intention" was not to harm, it was an accident. In this regard, every experience in the world, and every behavior is appropriate, given some context or some meaning frame. In this regard, we perhaps look at some aspect of ourselves differently. Again, is my behavior pure cussedness and being stubborn as a mule or is it courage and the ability to persevere in the face of adversity? It depends on context and the way we frame it.

It's important in changing our thinking to learn the skill of *Re-cognizing.* Let's look at some practical ways of changing some of our thinking and resultant self-talk.

I have been working with a young woman with an eating disorder (food addiction). We were discussing her self-image and I was trying to engage her in Re-Cognizing her self-talk. She stated in the simplest terms her self-image, "I am fat, stupid, and ugly." I encouraged her to dispute these as inaccurate over-generalizations. She said, "I can't because they are true." What to do? She really believes she is fat, stupid, and ugly. There was no way I could argue her out of it. So, I encouraged her to convince me, because I didn't see her in those terms, so I must be wrong in my view of her. She looked at me strangely, as if to say, "What game are you playing now?" So she began a litany of all the stupid things she had done, which were quite a few. Which of us can't come up with that kind of list? I can get suicidal in 10 minutes if I make a list of every stupid thing I have ever done. The point is, when we do this, we make it the whole picture. She was basing her self—image on her truth which excluded everything which did not fit.

I think the first thing which has to change is the perception we have of ourselves. If you treated your friends the way you treated yourself, would you have any friends? Learning to live with yourself means being willing to have a friendly, compassionate friendship with yourself. In order to do this, it involves forgiving yourself and accepting yourself. In a word—love yourself.

Now, listen to the way you talk to yourself. Is it the way a loving friend talks? I have encouraged you to write down labels and names. One of the most commonly accepted ways of countering self—criticism is to write down a negative thing and then counter it with positive self—affirmation. In her case, she wrote down stupid and then countered it with good student, active in a project to help teenagers with muscular dystrophy and a rather long list of accomplishments. Once this positive affirmation and its evidence is written down, the task is to invest it with positive emotion.

It is not enough to tell yourself you are not stupid and that you are really wonderful. It is more effective and realistic to focus on behavior. When we label our character we are global. By this I mean we assign all—inclusive labels that point to the way we are. For example, frequently used labels, fat, stupid, lazy, worthless, loser, bad, incompetent: the list is endless. These labels are destructive because they don't explain anything meaningfully. What does it tell us when she says "I am stupid?" It is more helpful if we focus realistically on behavior. An example of this is: I failed the exam because I did not adequately prepare and I don't have any real experience in this subject. This is a more realistic appraisal, and preserves self—esteem. It also leads to problem solving when you analyze what it is you need to do to pass the exam.

The statement, I am a loser can be countered several ways. If you are disappointed in yourself because you got passed over for a promotion, think it through. Get feedback, what is the boss looking for? How has your performance been? What did he tell you about why you were passed over?

Affirmations can be done in a number of ways. One is to make a list and carry it around. Another is to make a big sign and post it in a prominent place. Another is to make a tape recording and play it while you drive to work. Another is to have a friend make positive, affirming statements to you.

Here, in brief, is the short form for combating destructive, distorted thinking and talk.

(1) **Stop**—catch yourself in the act.

(2) **Identify** the emotion and ask yourself what you are doing to make yourself feel this way.

(3) **Verbalize** the distorted belief.

(4) **Step back**—disengage from the emotion. Relax!

(5) **Identify** the negative self—talk.

(6) **Dispute** it with contrary evidence and make countering

positive affirmations and coping statements. Practice this until it begins to feel natural.

We have covered a lot of territory in this chapter. We will be using it throughout the rest of the book. It is new, foreign, and feels unfamiliar and will take a while to get comfortable with the concepts. Practice, and success will help you integrate it into new ways of thinking, feeling and behaving. The following exercise will also help you get a better feel for the material we have introduced thus far.

NOTES

CHAPTER 5

THINKING—FEELING—BEHAVING

EXERCISE 1

In the following exercise, the goal is to begin integrating thinking, feeling and behaving. This will be done by learning to re—think situations through experiencing them in a new way.

Instructions

Take a few moments to visualize a situation which for you typically has created feelings of anger, sadness, fear, or depression. Visualize it as clearly as you can until you begin to feel what you customarily feel when in that situation.

Now we will apply the formula for dealing with these emotions.

Step 1   Name the Emotion

What ego state is operating?

Stop the action by telling yourself, firmly—**STOP!**

Step 2   Record

1. Describe in detail—in writing everything you know about this troublesome feeling. Remember to note: *before—during—after.* Also pay close attention to memories no matter how fragmentary they may seem.

2. Now! Write down your habitual thoughts—self—talk. Identify what you tell yourself. Identify key phrases that go with this feeling and situation.

147

Step 3   Identify the Belief

1.   Connect the situation with the ego state— emotion— self—talk with underlying belief.   What do you really believe about yourself— others—life?

Step 4   Assess the Belief

1. Put the emotion—self—talk and belief to the reality and validity check.

    1. Is it always true?

    2. What evidence do I have?

    3. Is it possible to see it a different way?

    4. What is the consequence of this belief to self—esteem?

    5. Is it rational or emotional?

    6. Whose rules are you applying?

    7. What would happen if everyone believed and felt this way?

Step 5   Re—cognize

1. Reframe the experience from several different perspectives. Develop the ability to detach and find alternate explanations.

2. Actively dispute distortions in thought with reality based statements.

3. Develop a list of positive affirmations directed at your self—esteem.

4. As your own best friend, make a prescription for change which will be compassionate and accepting.

CHAPTER 5

THINKING—FEELING—BELIEVING

EXERCISE 2

AFFIRM YOURSELF

Listed below are examples of affirmations which you may use or modify to suit your purposes. Remember to repeat them frequently and invest them with real meaning and feeling.

If you are targeting a particular belief— feeling—behavior write it down on a note card and then reinforce it with positive evidence of success.

1. I am responsible for my feelings.

2. I may not control everything but I can choose my attitude toward it.

3. I am competent.

4. I can take care of myself.

5. I am recovering.

6. I love and accept myself just the way I am.

7. I am committed to changing the things in my life which I do not like.

8. Every day I will do something to nurture me.

9. I do not need everyone to love me in order to feel good about me.

10. I am learning to build on my abilities and accomplishments.

11. I can take criticism and use it to my benefit.

12. I am taking risks daily to enrich myself.

13. I respect and believe in my right to be who I am.

14. I have a right to play and enjoy myself.

15. It is acceptable to make mistakes.

16. I have the right to feel all of my emotions.

17. I am willing to trust others.

18. I can be O.K. on my own.

19. I will become the kind of person I envision.

20. I am open to letting others love and support me.

EXERCISE 3

Listen to tape #3 Affirmations

NOTES

CHAPTER 5

THINKING—FEELING—BEHAVING

EXERCISE 4

GETTING TO KNOW YOUR CHILD

Listen to the tape entitled **The Inner Journey**. It is a guided imagery tape. Guided imagery is a technique that is successful in helping people get in touch with feelings and integrate them into their consciousness. It merely requires that you set aside 30 minutes where you will not be distracted and can completely relax.

After listening to the tape, spend some time writing down your experience and connecting with what you learned from it.

EXERCISE 5

Answer the following questionnaire which is designed to help you recognize some of your distorted beliefs. Rate each sentence on a 1—4 scale according to how much you think it influences your feelings and behavior. When you have completed it, go back and circle the ones you rated a 3 or 4.

Mistaken Beliefs Questionnaire

How much does each of these unconstructive beliefs influence your feelings and behavior? Take your time to reflect about each belief.

1 = **Not At All**   3 = **Strongly / frequently**
2 = **Somewhat/Sometimes** 4 = **Very Strongly**

Place the appropriate number after each statement:

1. I feel powerless or helpless.
2. Often I feel like a victim of outside circumstances.
3. I don't have the money to do what I really want.
4. There is seldom enough time to do what I want.
5. Life is very difficult—it's a struggle.
6. If things are going well, watch out!
7. I feel unworthy. I feel that I'm not good enough.
8. Often I feel that I don't deserve to be successful or happy.
9. Often I feel a sense of defeat and resignation: "Why bother!"

10. My condition seems hopeless.
11. There is something fundamentally wrong with me.
12. I feel ashamed of my condition.
13. If I take risks to get better, I'm afraid I'll fail.
14. If I take risks to get better, I'm afraid I'll succeed.
15. If I recovered fully, I might have to deal with realities I'd rather not face.
16. I feel like I'm nothing (or can't make it) unless I'm loved.
17. I can't stand being separated from others.
18. If a person I love doesn't love me in return, I feel like it's my fault.
19. It's very hard to be alone.
20. What others think of me is very important.
21. I feel personally threatened when criticized.
22. It's important to please others.
23. People won't like me if they see who I really am.
24. I need to keep up a front or others will see my weaknesses.
25. I have to achieve or produce something significant in order to feel O.K. about myself.
26. My accomplishments at work/school are extremely important.
27. Success is everything.
28. I have to be the best at what I do.
29. I have to be somebody—somebody outstanding.
30. To fail is terrible.
31. I can't rely on others for help.
32. I can't receive from others.
33. If I let someone get too close, I'm afraid of being controlled.
34. I can't tolerate being out of control.
35. I'm the only one who can solve my problems.
36. I should always be very generous and unselfish.
37. I should be the perfect... (rate each)
    a. employee   e. lover
    b. professional   f. friend
    c. spouse   g. student
    d. parent   h. son / daughter
38. I should be able to endure any hardship.
39. I should be able to find a quick solution to every problem.
40. I should never be tired or fatigued.
41. I should always be efficient.
42. I should always be competent.
43. I should always be able to foresee everything.
44. I should never be angry or irritable. Or: I don't like (or am afraid of) anger.
45. I should always be pleasant or nice no matter how I feel.

46. I often feel...(rate each)
    - a. guilty or ashamed   c. unintelligent
    - b. inferior or defective   d. ugly
47. I'm just the way I am—I can't really change.
48. The world outside is a dangerous place.
49. Unless you worry about a problem it just gets worse.
50. It's risky to trust people.
51. My problems will go away on their own with time.
52. I feel anxious about making mistakes.
53. I demand perfection of myself.
54. If I didn't have my safe person (or safe place), I'm afraid I couldn't cope.
55. If I stop worrying, I'm afraid something bad will happen.
56. I'm afraid to face the world out there on my own.
57. My self-worth isn't a given—it has to be earned.

You may have noticed that some of the beliefs on the questionnaire fall into special groups, each of which reflects a very basic belief or attitude toward life. Go back over your answers and see how you scored with respect to each of the groups of beliefs below.

Add up your scores for each subgroup of beliefs. If your total score on the items of a particular subgroup exceeds the criterion value, then this is likely to be a problem area for you. It's important that you give this group special attention when you begin to work with affirmations to start changing your mistaken beliefs.

SCORING

If your total score for questions 1, 2, 7, 9, 10, 11 is over 15:
You likely believe that you are powerless, have little or no control over outside circumstances, or are unable to do much that could help your situation. In sum, "I'm powerless" or "I can't do much about my life."

If your total score for questions 16, 17, 18, 19, 54, 56 is over 15:
You likely believe that your self—worth is dependent on the love of someone else. You feel that you need another's (or others') love to feel O.K. about yourself and to cope. In sum, "My worth and security are dependent on being loved."

If your total score for questions 20,21,22,23,24,45 is over 15:
You likely believe that your self—worth is dependent on others' approval. Being pleasing and getting acceptance from others is very important for your

sense of security and your sense of who you are. In sum, "My worth and security depend on the approval of others."

If your total score for questions 25, 26, 27, 28, 29, 30, 41, 42 is over 20
You likely believe that your self—worth is dependent on external achievements such as school or career performance, status, or wealth. In sum, "My worth is dependent on my performance or achievements."

If your total score for questions 31, 32,33,34,35,50 is over 15:
You likely believe that you can't trust, rely on, or receive help from others. You may have a tendency to keep a distance from people and avoid intimacy for fear of losing control. In sum, "If I trust or get too close, I'll lose control."

If your total score for questions 37, 38,39,40,52,53 is over 25:
You likely believe that you have to be perfect in some or many areas of life. You make excessive demands on yourself. There is no room for mistakes. In sum, "I have to be perfect" or "It's not O.K. to make mistakes."

This questionnaire was adapted from David Burns, M.D. Feeling Good chapter 10. See this book for more details on how to counter mistaken beliefs.

CHAPTER 5

THINKING, FEELING, BEHAVING

FURTHER READING

Burns, D.D.   The Feeling Good Handbook Using the New Mood Therapy in Everyday Life. New York: William Morrow. 1989.

Meichenbaum, D. Cognitive Behavior Modification.   An Integrative Approach. New York: Plenum Press 1977.

Seligman, Martin.   Learned Optimism.   New York: Simom & Shuster Inc. 1990.

NOTES

CHAPTER 6

SHAME & GUILT

Shame supposes that one is completely exposed and conscious of being looked at--in a word, self-conscious. One is visible and not ready to be visisble;...Shaming exploits the increased sense of being small.
Erik H. Erikson

In the previous chapter we focused primarily on the determining role of thinking as it related to feeling and behaving. In this chapter we will look at our feeling life, Particularlly with regard to the very difficult and often troublesome feelings of shame and guilt. As we have previously discussed, feelings provide that rich tapestry of human experience without which life would be a black and white film instead of technicolor. Additionally, we determined that the way that we experience and express our feelings is a marker of our identity. Let us, then, explore the role that feelings play in our psychological life and look at why such natural phenomena are often a source of perplexity and distress. Difficulties in the area of feelings usually fall into three categories: *experiencing, managing,* and *expressing.* For many people, the problem is not being able to experience their feelings or they don't know what they are feeling; being totally out of touch with themselves. One such category of individuals, usually male, have difficulty in feeling their feelings, as well as knowing what they feel. When asked, "what are you feeling right now?" it is very common for them to reply, "I don't know," or "nothing." Another kind of problem, but similar in many ways, is the engineering syndrome. I call it this because it is typical of men who are in the technical professions. When asked what they are feeling they respond with "I think." For them, feelings don't exist. They are so into their heads that they do not connect with their feeling life. Ironically, this kind of man usually marries a woman who is hysterical in nature. Of course, they both drive each other crazy. She complains, "he doesn't pay attention to my feelings." He complains, "I don't know what's the matter with her, she is so illogical." Each has married what is missing in themselves in order to balance their feeling life. Opposites do attract, but they also become a fertile source of conflict.

Why is it that people are so varied in their feeling responses? In order to answer this question, we have to make several observations about feelings.

The first thing we observe about feelings is that they are universal. Whether we are observing a primitive South American Indian Tribe or a group of New York Stock Brokers, we can see that all have feelings. What is different about their feelings is the mode of expression.

The second observation, then, is related to the first, we all have feelings but the patterning and expression of feelings is determined by social learning. Every society has rules about behavior; feelings are a part of these rules.

Some feelings are taboo, some can only be expressed in a narrow range, and some are appropriate between men and women, but not between men. Traveling in different cultures can be illuminating in this regard. As a foreigner, what we take for granted as normal and universal, can now be seen differently. Normal depends on local custom and cultural context.

To illustrate the importance of socialization in the shaping of emotions take a look at your own history. What was the emotional climate in your home? What feelings were permitted? What did you learn about your feelings and how they were to be expressed?

Again, an example from my own experience in regard to the powerful influences of parents on teaching children about feelings. My earliest memories of my father have to do with him teaching me about crying. His favorite response was, "Stop crying or I'll give you something to cry about." As an older child, he ridiculed and demeaned me for crying when we moved and I lost my friends. Though it was not his intent to teach me about feelings, he nevertheless had a profound influence on my ability to experience as well as express them. And since feelings are an integral part of us, parental responses toward our feelings also affect our self-esteem.

This leads to another observation about feelings; they are neutral except as they have come to have significance to others. For example, one of the most common problems clients of mine have is labeling their feelings good or bad. What I try to teach people is that feelings are neither good nor bad, they are just feelings. Once we can give ourselves permission to feel and take away the shoulds, it allows greater freedom to feel our feelings as well as greater freedom in their expression.

This brings us to another aspect of feelings. A question frequently asked is, "What good does it do to get angry?" What is the purpose or value of feelings? Feelings are of tremendous importance in our psychological makeup. They provide energy, motivation, and a sense of aliveness. Have you noticed how hard it is to get yourself to do anything if you don't feel like it? Feelings are also important because they are a byproduct of our ongoing experience. By this I mean they tell us important things from moment to moment as we live our lives.

Just as pain tells us something very important about the body, feelings do the same for the psyche. If we cut off our feelings we in fact have killed the messenger. We would never put our hand on a stove and tell ourselves, "I shouldn't feel this pain, I'm really not feeling anything." Feelings, then, not only tell us how we are feeling about our lives, but distress, anxiety, depression, sadness or anger may tell us also about what action we may need to take to resolve the distress.

In other words, distress tells us there is a problem and by heeding the message and deciphering its meaning we may then take decisive action to resolve the problem. I am working with a very "nice woman" who has trouble with anger. She continually says, "I got depressed for no reason the other day." This was said after her husband canceled a dinner invitation with some friends she likes but he can't stand. She did not make the connection between his behavior and her repressed anger, and so it turned into depression. Feelings are like light, there is a full spectrum ranging from euphoria to despair. Some are very enlivening and pleasant, others are so distressing as to lead to suicide in order to escape them. Usually feelings correspond well to how things are going in our lives.

This brings us to another observation about feelings. Since feelings are a natural response and a byproduct of experiencing, they affect not only the mind but also the body. In fact, it is not helpful to divide ourselves into body, mind, and emotions. We are in fact a totality. For this reason, when we do not permit ourselves to experience or express our emotions they must be expressed somehow. This is where symptom formation comes in.

Feelings which are not expressed, are suppressed, avoided, or become expressed in some other way. This was the great discovery of Freud. Depression, anxiety, panic attacks, as well as a multitude of psychosomatic illnesses all are testament to the power of feelings which are not permitted primary expression. On the more subtle level we find that not dealing with feelings leaves people feeling dead, empty, bored or restless. These are the symptoms of distress which often lead people to seek psychotherapy. They do not understand their feelings and therefore the meaning of their discomfort.

In the previous chapters we have explored the topics of stress and looked at childhood origins in order to understand some of the problems in living people develop. Many of these stem from painful experiences which have left emotional scars. Trauma, ineffective parenting and other painful experiences leave their legacy. As a result we have problems in feeling and identifying our feelings as well as adequate means of managing and expressing them. Many of these difficulties have arisen because of shame and guilt regarding our emotions.

Generally, feelings are divided into simple (primary) and complex (secondary). Primary emotions are anger, sadness, joy, sexuality, pleasure and fear. They are regarded as primary because infants exhibit them without social learning. The complex emotions refer to feelings which are mixed or are ones which we experience as a reaction to feeling a primary feeling. An example might be the feelings one experiences over the death of a friend who has suffered during a long illness. We can feel relief, sadness, anger, guilt and fear all at the same time.

In the rest of this chapter we will discuss shame and guilt and in subsequent chapters other difficult emotions. I have chosen to discuss shame and guilt first because of their prominent role in influencing the way we experience as well as express all of our other feelings.

SHAME

It is very common for most people to group shame and guilt together. They, however, are not the same. They are similar in that they often result in a person's feeling badly about something but are different in their developmental origins. Shame is related to feeling inferior and originates at an earlier developmental period. Guilt has to do with transgression. I have included these two concepts for discussion together because they have to do with autonomy and self—regulation; or in simpler terms, standing on one's own two feet and controlling one's impulses. Shame and guilt are two of the most common problems which surface in treatment. Often of longstanding and deeply rooted origin, shame and guilt cause people to feel very badly about themselves. These lowered feelings of self—esteem are reflected in much self—hatred and self—destructive behavior, and the inability to feel anything at all.

Let us explore these two similarly complex, powerful, and troubling experiences. It is important to our understanding in that they have many implications for self—esteem. Most importantly, we will try to find ways to unburden the self from shame and guilt and thereby more comfortable in our emotional expression. One cannot move toward the goal of empowerment without unlocking the shackles of shame and guilt.

Basically the goal is to develop a more compassionate way of looking at one's self by understanding the role that shame and guilt have distorted relationships with others and the self. The result of shame and guilt is to have a poor, often hateful relationship with self and others. The antidote for shame and guilt is forgiveness and reconciliation: forgiveness of oneself and reconciliation with others. But it cannot happen until we become reconciled to ourselves.

Shame, in my view, occurs in human development at an earlier stage than guilt. It occurs concurrently with the emergence of autonomy, which begins at birth and becomes fully an issue by age 4. As the self emerges there is a dawning awareness of separateness from others. This consciousness of self begins with the development of language and the growth of the body. As the child begins to experience the power of controlling the bodily functions and acquires mastery over walking, talking, eating, and elimination, he/she is also learning that this emergent independence has an impact on others.

This developmental period is known by most parents as the "terrible two's." The child has learned the power of negation. Saying no means to stand in opposition to others. The child is not only learning to stand on his/her own two feet, literally, but is also learning to stand up to others. In any critical period of human development there is a great deal of vulnerability. The vulnerability at this stage is twofold. What is at risk is the child's sense of self and the tenuous relationship with others. The child in obeying the biological urges to grow is standing on a crucial bridge to others. How they respond to this new development is important to the child's self—esteem. The conflict at this stage is between the need for mastery and the need for approval. The child experiences simultaneously the joy of willing, acting, choosing, and freedom with the need to be validated and have the significant adults mirror those same feelings of satisfaction and gladness. As if to say, "yes, we too are glad you are growing and are happy for you to become more independent."

If the emerging independence is praised, supported, and nurtured, there is a gain in confidence. If the child is shamed, humiliated or embarrassed, there is an acute lowering of self—esteem. Shame feels like an internal hemorrhage. The child is aware of being small, helpless, dependent, and somehow defective in character. The shame family of emotions range in severity from shyness, bashfulness, and feeling self—conscious to the more harmful feelings of being demeaned, debased, disgraced and thought of as contemptible. The determinant of course, here, is the strength of the parental reprimand. Criticism may be delivered with tolerance and warmth or with cruelty, hostility and rejection. It is the quality of the response which is important because the parental response with all of its feeling intensity becomes internalized and then becomes a part of the child's reaction patterns.

Being shamed clusters around several basic issues. These issues often have their origin in unresolved parental conflicts over these same issues: the issues pertain to weakness, incompetence, control, dependency, and perfectionism. Criticism or censure from a parent comes as a powerful stimulus to a child. Shame when it enters the relationship cuts like a dual—edged sword. It comes as an immediate sense of inadequacy and at the same time a feeling of loss of that all important affectionate bond with the parent. The net consequence of shame for the child may be

165

formulated as "I have lost your love because there is something wrong with me." This threat of abandonment unleashes very powerful and primitive anxiety. Shame is the feeling of being exposed in all of one's terrible inadequacy; of being unable to hide these apparently unlovable qualities.

Shame can paralyze. It can turn off emotion and prevent the expression of any sense of the self. For the sensitive child it may lead to being chronically apologetic, meek, and excessively approval seeking. In adulthood, shame may be manifested as an inability to carry out and plan any form of independent action. It is also reflected in harsh and punitive self—criticism. For shame is linked to our entire concept of what it is to be lovable as adults. Rooted in these earlier experiences of shame the adult's independence and self—esteem is undermined.

A case from my clinical practice comes to mind which seems to best illustrate the problems based in a chronic sense of shame. My client, a 38—year—old woman was referred to therapy by her lawyer. She was complaining of depression and marital problems. She was married to a successful man, lived in a nice house and had three beautiful children. (the American Dream). But she was not happy. She stated, "my life's a mess, I'm totally confused, I don't know what I want, I can't seem to get any enjoyment out of anything. My husband doesn't love me, my kids resent me, my parents think I'm stupid and should just grow up. No matter what I do, it ends up the same way, I'm miserable and I hate myself. I feel so damned stupid and incompetent."

166

Feeling incompetent, defective and embarrassed about herself, she had all of the symptoms of shame. My client was raised in a large family by two parents, both of whom she describes as alcoholics. "Mother never had time for me and dad was always traveling." Though she did well in school, she felt it was never good enough. This pervasive feeling affects all of her endeavors. No matter what she does, it's not good enough. Translated, I'm not good enough. The problem of shame undermines self—esteem, she also feels defective in relationships and feels "unloved". Because of a tremendous hunger for affection she tries desperately to please others. She is over—compliant, nice, bends over backwards to do for others and wonders why no one ever does anything for her. Because she is so desperate to please she over gives, over commits and is chronically overwhelmed. Financially, her life is a mess because she cannot manage her affairs. In sum, she disappoints herself and resents others. She struggles desperately to overcome her depression but fears that she won't be able to do that right either. She "just hates her life."

If shame leads to feeling defective, exposed, vulnerable, and unable to love and be loved, what is the antidote? The solution to this problem must begin with recognition that it is a serious problem. The solution to this problem can be complicated and difficult to resolve because so much damage has been done to the self at such a vulnerable age. But basically, the goal is to regain a sense of validity and legitimacy. To learn to love oneself.

The journey from shame to legitimacy goes through the valley of despair. For the first encounter with shame is often depressing. As we encounter very early and painful memories it can be quite oveerwhelming. As we search for the love we never got as a child, the despair threatens to engulf. To recognize this painful state as we realistically appraise our parents means we must break through the denial and tendency to idealize them. To work through the pain is to feel the full force of the lovelessness of ones life. It often turns out in this encounter that "I didn't feel loved then, and I have been searching ever since for the love that I missed."

Once the journey has begun with awareness of the problem, despair may now be transformed into the doorway to freedom. This use of despair will be explored more fully in the next section. However, for now, despair must be confronted because it is the key to unlocking the problem of shame. To overcome this problem, a person must do two things. The first is to confront the feeling of being defective. Only you can give yourself the right to be. Secondly, a new relationship with yourself must begin. One that is based on acceptance, understanding, forgiveness, and compassion. In essence, the most difficult task of all is learning to love ourselves in spite of never having been loved. We must teach ourselves how to love. No one can do this for us. We are the problem and the solution. Who can give us a sense of legitimacy and validity but us? All to often we pursue the illusory idea that if I can just find the right person to love me, then I will be okay. This illusion leads to disillusionment because no one can love another person enough to fill the void caused by shame. In fact, shame prevents us from feeling the love we so desperately desire because we feel so unworthy.

In summary, shame is an experience of lost approval that leads to a complex blend of experiences which at the core caused the self to feel devalued and exposed. It originates in the earliest of developmental stages where the child is emerging as a separate human being testing his/her power and autonomy. Shame affects the ability to value the self and also the critical interpersonal bridge of shared esteem with others. Shame when it becomes a part of the self's enduring relationship with itself may be triggered by any criticism, disappointment or perceived failure. Finally, shame turns the self against itself. It limits self—love and is characterized by perpetual self—contempt. All of this because in our state of being small, dependent, incompetent and defenseless we were ridiculed and demeaned: it is the failure to love at an elemental level.

GUILT

Getting along in society means being able to meet one's needs while being sensitive to the social situations around one and governing oneself accordingly. This self—governing capability is learned through the socializing influence of family and school. These become the primary social agencies responsible for transmitting societies values. Moral development goes hand in hand with the emotional, social and intellectual development of a child. Development of a conscience is a much more complex process than just learning a set of rules and teaching a child to feel badly when he/she violates them. Moral development includes in its most basic form the ability to discriminate between right and wrong, but it also includes the more complex abilities of perceiving and being sensitive to the needs of others (empathy). It also means being able to establish routines and accepting responsibility for personal actions. Learning to discriminate various social roles and how to interact properly with others is also an important aspect. In its most highly developed state, moral development means becoming aware of cooperative and interdependent relationships which are necessary for the greater good of others and society. These are abstract moral principles which often transcend rules and law. For example, Nazi Guards who obeyed orders to execute prisoners were acting within the law of their land, but were violating higher moral principles.

Moral development is a complex social learning process which goes through several stages. The experience of guilt also goes through the same process. It is intricately tied to the socialization practices of parents and other adult authority figures. Guilt is the byproduct of moral development. It reflects how the socialization process has become internalized and the quality of the moral sense.

Historically, psychology has treated this development as superego formation. This is a term which is used to describe the socialization process which leads to being capable of self—governing. In essence, the superego is the internalized values of a culture as it finds its expression in an individual conscience. In simple terms, it is easiest to think of conscience as the internal voice of one's parents. The net effect of the superego is that we treat ourselves the way we were treated. In this regard it is important to understand the ways your parents disciplined you, responded to your mistakes, and failures, and misbehavior. Quite often, a great deal of work in therapy is in reworking the superego.

If the quality of the superego is harsh, critical, demeaning, impatient, and judgmental, in short a tyrant, then the task is formidable. Each of us must, finally, if we are to live with any contentment, learn to develop our own values, govern ourselves, and learn to be compassionate with our failings.

Guilt and moral development do not necessarily progress in a smooth line through the developmental stages. They are subject to the same processes of human development as the other matters we have been considering. Guilt and moral development may get stuck at a particular level or become perverse in its manifestation because of the context in which it was learned. When this occurs, the child may have serious problems in self—regulation, knowing appropriate social behavior, aggression, anti—social behavior, or of being unable to engage in cooperative behavior with others.

Those who do not conform to societies rules are labeled "deviant". Society has many systems for those who are unable

171

to fit in. Those who do not go by the rules may be ostracized, or may be placed in penal institutions or hospitalized for mental illness. For many others there is another kind of prison. This prison is replete with its own penalties and tortures: the prison of guilt. Those who suffer from unremitting guilt have become their own policemen, judge, jury and executioner. These individuals are far more severe with their sentencing than anything society would impose.

Let us examine some of the factors involved in the development of conscience and see what occurs when moral development goes off course.

Moral development does not occur in a systematic and well ordered fashion. Socialization occurs informally within a family system through regular, or irregular daily activities. The adequacy of learning is determined by the kind and quality of the family structure, the marital relationship and the emotional climate within the home. Each family has a unique style which is an outgrowth of the parental personalities.

Two parental qualities are important in the socialization of the child. The first has to do with control. How the parent transmits rules depends upon how comfortable that parent is with control and being controlled. (Authority) Parents vary with regard to the degree that they are "authoritarian or democratic" in their treatment of misbehavior. The authoritarian parent makes the child conform to absolute standards of conduct and enforces the rules with punishment and expects unquestioned obedience. The authoritarian parent does not explain the reasons for rules nor the possible consequences of the behavior in question. The child is not consulted by the parent for opinions and is not taken into consideration in family plans. All power resides with the parents. This concern with strict control often results in a detached relationship with the children who tend to be discontent, withdrawn, conforming and low in self—esteem.

Democratic parents on the other hand, are warm and accepting with the child. They help the child toward independence and explain the basis of rules and consequences of the child's actions. Power is shared between parent and child in the democratic family structure. Rules and values are transmitted in a flexible manner subject to modification and discussion depending on the situation. The impact of this kind of parenting is a more self—reliant child who is more confident and higher in self—esteem. The child is also capable of greater self—control and cooperation with others. The second parental characteristic which is important to the child's development is that of nurturance. Again, this is not an absolute quality. Parents vary with regard to the degree they manifest this quality. They range from one extreme which is hostile, cold, cruel, and rejecting to the other end of the spectrum which is highly accepting, caring and warmly affectionate. In most child development studies, this is the quality found to be most important to the healthy emotional development of the child.

The development of a conscience, or moral sensitivity goes through three stages of development. We may characterize these stages as *Corporal,* *Conventional,* and *Ethical.*

Childhood encompasses the Corporal stage which is typified by fear of punishment and a concrete understanding of rules. Because the child understands everything from an ego—centric point of view, his/her interpretation of rules is also highly personal. There is very little understanding of consequences or the impact of behavior on others. Rules are absolute and the child is incapable of abstract moral reasoning because of cognitive development.

The second phase is associated with late childhood and adolescence. Moral development at this stage is highly conventional. The adolescent conforms because everyone else does it that way. Morality is related to the need to belong and values reflect the dominant values of that culture.

Finally, in the ethical stage, a person's behavior is governed by adherence to abstract, general principles which have become internalized. Personal moral values are steadfastly adhered to even when they are sometimes in conflict with established laws and social order. An example of this is found in a person who might steal a drug to preserve a human life. In this person's view, preserving life is a higher moral obligation than not stealing.

Not everyone passes through these developmental stages inevitably like physical development. It is quite obvious from experience that moral development occurs quite unevenly. Some acquire high degrees of moral sensitivity, others maintain a Corporal position. Others go through life with very Conventional values. Still others are sociopathic in their orientation (being anti—social or having no regard for human values other than their own). What is of consequence for our discussion is how this socialization process affects the individual and how each person has come to behave in the moral sphere. The critical issue in shame and guilt is the end product of socialization. Shame as we discussed previously has to do with how one regards oneself. Whether one feels that one has the right to be. Guilt has to do with transgression of rules or values; how one goes about being and the values which guide and sustain meaningful behavior.

Just as shame is a central factor in the development of autonomy, guilt is primary in self—control. Guilt is a sense of having transgressed, of violating some written or unwritten code. When guilt is experienced, it is often totally out of proportion to what was actually done. In fact, some people feel guilt for things which have little or no connection to morality.

For example, a client of mine who is a middle aged man uses in the space of five sentences the word should ten times. "I should do this, I should do that, I should've done that, should, should, should, etc.." He shoulds himself to death. He has developed a very severe conscience which leaves him very little room for spontaneous action. His conscience won't leave him alone. He feels guilty for the smallest transgressions. For a "wrong thought", for "being too selfish," for being angry with his wife who "deserted him and his schizophrenic son, he punishes himself endlessly. This guilt leads to excessive self—criticism, it contaminates every emotion, thought and behavior.

This self—punitive, self—hating attitude keeps him chronically depressed and unhappy, his self—esteem remains low. As a result, he feels he doesn't deserve anything good happening to him. We ask, how does this occur? My client is the third son of an alcoholic father and a depressed and abused mother. He also was physically and emotionally abused by his father. As a boy, nothing ever was good enough for his father. The rigid perfectionism of the father led to punishment and continual angry rebuke. All of this was internalized by my client, particularly the hostile, rejecting attitude.

In sum, my client now treats himself just like his father treated him. This is the general rule in guilt. It's as if he has never been able to get his father off his back. We may see, then, that guilt leads to excessive self—criticism and punishment. It results in low self—esteem and blocks emotion and spontaneous activity. In relationships with others it often leads to feeling one down (the underdog position.) Guilty people don't feel as if they have any rights. And guilt leads to projection. A process by which we attribute our own unconscious feelings and motives onto other people. In this case, my client often feels other men are hostile and critical of him; demanding just like his father.

It is evident that he is fixated or stuck in the first stage of moral development. His behavior is controlled by the fear of punishment. Only now, it is strictly an internal struggle. He is both the punisher and the punished. Several things must take place for him to make progress in reducing his guilt. The first work which must be done is on the relationship with his father. The goal is not to affix blame, but rather to understand how this relationship was formative to his feelings about himself. Formative, in that most often one treats oneself like one was treated as a child. Therefore, relationships, including with oneself, frequently are a reenactment of the original parent child drama. Once the feelings about this relationship are explored, clarified and understood, then the feelings about the parent may be released. Only then may the wounds begin to heal. Many people have found a curious thing happening. As they forgive and accept their parents they are able to have a much more compassionate relationship with themselves.

A necessary step in working through this relationship is to become aware of the language that was used by the parents in correcting the child. As adults, we use the same language toward ourselves. This self—talk is the inner language of the self. It is a constant dialogue about the ongoing process of daily living. If this language is critical, self— blaming, and hostile or demeaning, as it usually is, it must be changed. In the exercises at the end of the previous chapter you were given instructions on how to deal with this self—talk, The goal is to develop a more compassionate, less guilty, more affirming relationship with self and others. Go back and review the language with regard to shame and guilt.

Finally, to alleviate the problem of guilt, there must be a new formulation of values. It is time to stop blaming yourself, to stop living by all of the old shoulds and hand me down values. In order to do this one must question all the old shoulds you have been living by. Most people live unconsciously, and have not seriously questioned their shoulds. The question is do they work for you? Do they give your life purpose, meaning and direction? These are important questions to ask yourself. Not all shoulds are wrong. What is important is to come to terms with the oughts and rules in your life and make them your own. When they become your own you will feel more like living by them. And then, if you violate your own credo, then you can decide rationally what to do about it. Either change the credo or change the behavior. At least the guilt will serve a useful purpose. Rather than a form of self—abuse and self—reproach, it can be a tool for self—correction and self—governing as it should be. A tool to help you live the way you want to; on your own terms.

NOTES

CHAPTER 6

SHAME AND GUILT

EXERCISE 1

Write a letter to your parent or parents that you seem to associate with the most guilt. In this letter, express everything you feel— no need to censor it. Express all your regret, resentment, hurt and unmet needs. Let yourself freely feel and express it deeply. You may feel whatever you feel. There is no need to protect them or feel guilt for the way you feel. This letter is for you. This is not for publication. You may share it with them or not. It is to help you finish up any unfinished business you may have with them. This is to help you clarify and identify our feelings and uncover the source of your shame and guilt.

EXERCISE 2

Write a declaration of independence. This is your 4th of July. Now that you have declared your independence, the next step is to write a Bill of Rights. In this Bill of Rights give yourself permission to be the kind of person you want to be. Finally, define your own terms. How do you want to live? What is your new Credo? Will it help you bring your life to fruition?

SHAME AND GUILT

EXERCISE 3

FEEL YOUR FEELINGS! In order to begin connecting with yourself it is important to feel your feelings. Set aside a few moments. Stop the action—ask yourself "What am I feeling right now?" Don't be misled if you think you are not feeling anything. Begin a few sentences with **Right now I am aware of _____ and then just say what you are aware of.**

Examples:

> Right now I am aware of writing this chapter.
>
> I am aware of tiredness.
>
> I feel too warm.
>
> I am aware of the radio playing my favorite music.
>
> I am aware of the traffic noise etc..

CHAPTER 6

SHAME AND GUILT

EXERCISE 4

SELF—MONITORING. Periodically, throughout the day stop and ask yourself— "What am I experiencing right now?" Focus your attention on what you are engaged in. What does it feel like?

EXERCISE 5

Have a discussion with someone about something you have strong feelings about. Tell them about it. Describe how you feel to that person. Then listen to them talk about a feeling. What are you aware of?

CHAPTER 6

SHAME AND GUILT

FURTHER READING

Bradshaw, John. Homecoming: Reclaiming and Championing Your Inner Child. New York: Bantam Books. 1990.

Erikson, Erik H. Identity, Youth and Crisis. New York: Norton & Co. Inc., 1968

Madow, Leo. Guilt: How to Recognize and Cope With It. New Jersey: Jason Aronson, Inc., 1988.

DEPRESSION & ANXIETY

What is there? I know first of all that I am. But who am I? All I know of myself is that I suffer. And if I suffer it is because at the origin of myself there is mutilation, separation. I am separated. What I am separated from--I cannot name it. But I am separated. Formerly it was called God. Today it no longer has any name.

                                                        Arthur Adamov

My phone rang very early one morning six years ago. It was one of my friends, a former professor, calling to inform me that a friend and colleague had committed suicide the day before. In shock, anger and confusion, I said something exasperated like, "I didn't even know he was depressed." Suicide is one manifestation of depression; a malady that is the number one mental health problem today. Depression is a complex and often paradoxical problem for which many people do not even seek treatment. In my friend's case, he was apparently "successful", had a group of long time friends, a beautiful and also "successful" wife, was loved and respected by his clients, and had achieved professional stature in the community. Yet, seemingly out of the blue he ended his life.

Depression appears in many ways to all kinds of people. Deeply rooted in the universal human condition, records of melancholy and despair are found in the earliest recorded accounts of man's experience. Depression affects all ages, races, occupations, and socio-economic classes. Everyone at one time or another has probably felt the numbing, deadening, painfully helpless, sense of hopelessness and despair that comes with a loss or a disappointment. This transitory experience comes with the ups and downs in life; the "slings and arrows of outrageous fortune." No one is immune, however, some people appear to be more vulnerable to depression and loss than others. For these people, depression is not a sometimes occurring, unwelcome visitor. Depression arrives like an unwanted relative who comes to stay a week and moves in and totally disrupts the household. This kind of depression can become disabling; a progressively deteriorating problem leading to serious impairment in the ability to carry out the daily affairs of life. A common complaint with this kind of depression is: "I don't know why I feel this way, I have everything, but I just can't seem to shake this feeling of doom and gloom."

Depression has many masks. Its symptoms are varied in severity as well as forms of expression. Despite its many faces, however, depression does have several symptoms which appear to cluster together into a recognizable syndrome.

The usual or essential features of depression are a loss of pleasure or interest in all or almost all of a person's usual activities. This condition is quite persistent over a period of time, usually three to six months. It is also associated with disturbances in appetite and sleep. In heavy people, appetite increases, and in thin people appetite decreases. It doesn't seem fair, does it? There is also a change in energy, some people feel agitated and others feel lethargic. Also noted are changes in thinking with problems in memory, concentration, and often persistent, morbid and melancholic thoughts of worthlessness and suicide. A feeling of guilt, leading to withdrawal from life is common. A person may experience some, or in extreme cases, all of these signs.

Depression in children and adolescents may be expressed by changes in personality and behavior. School performance usually declines, and relationships with teachers and peers often deteriorate. It is very common for adolescents to "act their depression out" in anti-social, rebellious, or self-destructive activity. In young children depression often manifests itself in fears, nightmares and physical ailments and complaints. There may also be a general regression to previous levels of development, like bedwetting and soiling.

Depression may also disguise itself in features that one would not ordinarily think of as depression. Such as health problems, physical distress, irritability, fears, brooding, worry, panic attacks, phobias and insomnia. One person, for example, was referred to me by a cardiologist because of chest pains, rapid pulse and shortness of breath. She had a complete cardiac workup and nothing physically wrong was found, hence the psychological referral. This is often a difficult referral because the individual has the physical symptoms and may resent the implication that they are "crazy". Once I saw this person and reassured her that the referral didn't mean that her physician thought she was "crazy", together we were able to discover that she had been suffering from depression for years.

In sum, depression is a disorder which may be manifested by disturbances in thought, feeling and behavior. It also affects the physical functioning of the body. In some individuals it affects only one domain, and in others it may involve all. In the mental health profession there are many models for understanding and classifying depression. They reflect the diversity of opinion that goes with the complexity of the problem.

There are disease models which emphasize the underlying bio—chemical nature of depression. One of my friends, a neuro—physiological—psychologist keeps telling me that the need for psychotherapy will be obsolete once they fully understand the brain chemistry and processes of depression. He represents one end of the philosophical debate. At the other end of the spectrum are the cognitive behavioral psychologists who believe that depression is a learned problem of faulty perception and thoughts which lead to depressive behaviors. This debate is endless and could fill volumes. For purposes of our discussion and the sake of simplification, we will concentrate on the psychological factors which have been found to be of significance in the causes of depression.

In my model, I prefer to accept that there are possible bio—chemical predisposing factors which interact with learning and social stressors. What is central, in my view, is discovering the meaning depression has for a particular person. This is done by investigating the roots of depression as it relates to a person's particular history. Once the history is understood, usually the meaning of the depression is perfectly understandable. And it has been my experience that once the history is understood what comes of this process is that I am able to see the world through my client's eyes.

In order to unravel the complexities of depression in real life, one must look to the total picture presented by the sufferer. Depression, when looked at in totality, is a signal that is to the psyche what pain is to the body. It is a distress signal indicating that a person is suffering from psychological malnutrition.   Just as joy and pleasure are byproducts of pleasurable activities, so, likewise depression is a byproduct of interactions that leave the self feeling depleted, exhausted, numb, helpless and hopeless.

To return for a moment to our discussion on identity: depression is a result of an individual's inability to maintain self—esteem.   By looking at depression from this perspective, we may see that it stems from the very roots of human personality.

When the needs for competence, significance, and meaning are not met, depression is the inevitable result.   This point is well illustrated by the death of my friend.   He had a severely abusive father and a mother who was distant and cold. He based his whole life (self—esteem project) on achieving his dream of success.   In other people's eyes he had "made it". But the dream did not fill his emptiness.   No matter how much he achieved, it was not enough.   He was still not pleased with himself.   In fact, the more he achieved the more guilty he felt for surpassing his father.   The critical internalized father would not let him enjoy his success.   To quell his pain, he used drugs and alcohol. His suicide indicated to me both an internal collapse of his identity as well as a belief that there was nothing he could do to make any difference.

This, of course, became a solution that turned into another way to feel bad. This worsened his feelings of self—contempt and guilt. Finally, the body began to break down under the stress and abuse. He became ill from a virus. Emotionally depleted and physically ill, the internal struggle to appear normal became too great. His collapsing world went unnoticed by wife and friends. Seeking help would have been too great an admission of defeat to his self—esteem. He chose what he felt was his final and only option: suicide!

Current stress, vulnerability, low self—esteem, and old unhealed wounds did him in. The need to feel powerful, to be loved, to love ourselves, and to feel that our lives mean something are the most powerful of human needs. Deprived of these, few of us would feel like continuing to struggle. When they are not fulfilled and the possibility of meeting them appears futile, depression is the necessary consequence. When depression signals the failure of the self project, it is imperative that the message is received. Depression signals a need for a remedy.

Strategies for recovery must come from a careful understanding of the meaning of depression. To follow the model we developed in previous sections, we must first analyze the problem. By tracing the depression to its roots, we will no doubt find the problem to be in the early relationships where self—esteem begins. This early damage to self is often painful and difficult to heal. In our work on self-esteem, shame and guilt, we made a good beginning. Work must continue on healing those early wounds while at the same time addressing present problems in living. Many of my clients complain that this is the most difficult part of therapy. It's like trying to live in a house while undergoing a complete remodel.

Depression is paradoxical in that it requires a tremendous effort from someone who often doesn't feel like caring or trying. So the first and most important thing is to try to do something; make an effort. Start somewhere! No matter how small the beginning, it is important to take control over even little things. It can feel so overwhelming! It is necessary to get moving. Perhaps taking a walk daily; washing the car; cleaning one room of the house, etc... It is vital to restore lost routines and rebuild healthy activities which restore a sense of control and competence. Secondly, stop criticizing yourself. You must begin a systematic program of loving self-care. Each day you must do something which will make you feel better about yourself. The negative self-talk which perpetuates depression must be changed, as well as your basic outlook on life which views the world depressively.

Finally, I would like to suggest a structured approach to changing some of those negative and self-destructive thoughts which perpetuate depression. We will focus specifically on thoughts and behaviors that are linked to your depression.

Step One: Identify the connection between a depressing thought and the feeling of melancholy, depression or sadness.

The thought can be something like: "I don't deserve to be happy," or nobody will ever love me." Or, another depresive thought which reflects feelings of helplessness: "nothing I do matters, so it won't do any good to try."

Step Two: Notice the sequence between the thoughts and an immediate lowering in motivation, energy and a tendency to withdraw. Observe how you change your mood and behavior by the kinds of thoughts you think and the things you tell yourself about what is going to happen. Understanding this process of thought and expectation is crucial to dealing with depression.

Step Three: Take time to explore all of the depressing thoughts you use. Make a list of them. Create a hall of fame for depressing thoughts. What are the all time crunchers you use to make yourself feel really bad?

Step Four: Now that you have made a list of these all time greats, stop and really look at them. Own them as your thoughts and something you have control over. Now, ask yourself, "Are they true?" Are they factually based? Where did you get these ideas about yourself and the world? Evaluate these thoughts for their errors and their source: use the paradigm from chapter 5.

Step Five: Break the errors in thought down. Is it true that you have always been a failure, all the time? You have *never* done anything right? You have *never* been happy? Remember always and never are over–generalizations which frequently cause depression. Another of my favorite logical errors is catastrophizing. This is the "Chicken Little

Syndrome." Every little thing that goes wrong becomes a sign that the world is coming to an end. For example, I can't find a clean shirt, therefore, I think, this is going to be a terrible day. See if you can identify ones that you use.

Step Six: Notice that all of these logical errors are based on an underlying assumption. See if you can spot the underlying belief in "I have always been a loser." This is based on the belief, "I am no good." Someone who cannot do anything right doesn't deserve anything good to happen to them, right? This set of beliefs also predicts the future and makes it come true. "I am a loser and will always be a loser" is a self—fulfilling prophecy that we make come true through our beliefs and actions.

Step Seven: Examine and evaluate your basic assumptions about yourself and life. What do you really believe is true about you, other people, and life in general? Check these ideas out for accuracy. Notice what they reveal about your basic self-schema.

Step Eight: Now that you have taken a good look at some of the thoughts which lead to and reinforce depression, it is time to pick one specific thing you do which keeps you depressed. Having a very specific target for change will focus your effort and make success in changing that much easier to observe. Write it down and get very specific about how it works, when it works, and how it is reinforced or rewarded. What is the payoff for this particular behavior? Does it work? In the concluding exercise section we will be providing several exercises to help you in this regard.

In conclusion, depression is an important signal which, when the meaning is discovered, may lead to a long needed recovery of self—esteem, competence, and restored relationships with yourself and others. Depression may stem from a loss of things which one deems necessary to maintain security and safety; or it may mean that one is experiencing a sense of futility in meeting basic needs such as love, affection, and support from significant others. Finally, depression may mean that one is reenacting a problem in the present which has roots in early childhood. This reenactment may trigger very powerful and long repressed hurts, memories and feelings. Whatever the trigger to depression, it requires effort to work it through to healing.

Remember the model we have been using which is based on **Awareness, Assessment, and Action.** This model leads to self—empowerment which is the logical antidote to depression. If depression is a symptom of devalued self—esteem, loss of significance and meaning, alienation from others, and a sense of futility and helplessness then self—empowerment will lead to healing not only of the mind and spirit but also of the body. This is where it is crucial to discover and unleash the hidden healer residing within all of us.

ANXIETY

Many of the things which have been written about depression may also be true of anxiety. In fact, anxiety and depression often coincide. Anxiety is a disorder which affects approximately 5% of the population. The most common quality associated with anxiety is that people often try to cope with it by resorting to the use of central nervous system depressants such as alcohol and tranquilizers. As we have discussed, this connection frequently begins the process of chemical dependence. A solution which becomes a problem. In fact, the biggest problem with anxiety is that it leads to so many avoidance behaviors.

Anxiety is characterized by feelings of acute discomfort, apprehension, fearfulness, tension, and numerous somatic sensations. These may include several of the following: hot and cold flashes, dizziness, faintness, weakness, sweating, numbness, tingling sensations, muscle paralysis, heart palpitations, chest pain, shortness of breath, feelings of unreality, choking, a large lump in the throat, and a dread of catastrophe.

Whereas depression causes a slowing or numbing of feeling, behavior, and thinking, anxiety usually is manifested by central nervous system hyperactivity. Most people prefer depression to anxiety because depression does not threaten a loss of control. Because in anxiety there is an overarousal of the central nervous system, chemicals which depress the activity have very reinforcing properties. They help a person feel more comfortable and at the same time perpetuate avoidance.

Again, like depression, anxiety affects all ages and no one is immune from feeling anxious or fearful at times. Generally, anxiety symptoms are categorized into three classes. The first class of symptoms are **phobias**. In this category, anxiety is limited to fear of specific objects with specific avoidance patterns a person utilizes to control the anxiety. Fear of animals, closed spaces and public embarrassment are common phobias. For most people, this is not a very serious or disabling disorder because the specific situations or objects are easily avoided. These phobias often have their origins in childhood experiences or are a result of conditioning.

A second order of anxiety is the *generalized variety*. This is anxiety without a specific focus or more of a vague or free floating quality. Because the sufferer in this case is not able to locate the cause so easily, it is generally more difficult to accommodate oneself to this problem.

Generalized anxiety has historically been treated as a problem emerging from within the person's unconscious. As such, it usually stems from repression of early childhood trauma, and conflict over discharge of intense feelings and impulses. Much of the work done in earlier sections has focused on these experiences. It is often difficult to know what it is exactly that is making us anxious because the signal of anxiety may be the result of very complex experiences. For example, a few years ago I was at the dentist having my teeth cleaned and during the procedure I became so anxious that I broke into a cold sweat, felt incredibly trapped and immediately nauseous.

It was so intolerable, I had to leave. What was the meaning of this experience? This is the foremost question which comes to mind. If anxiety is an alarm signal, where was the danger? I was in a dentist's chair being cared for by a

A COGNITIVE MODEL OF DEPRESSION

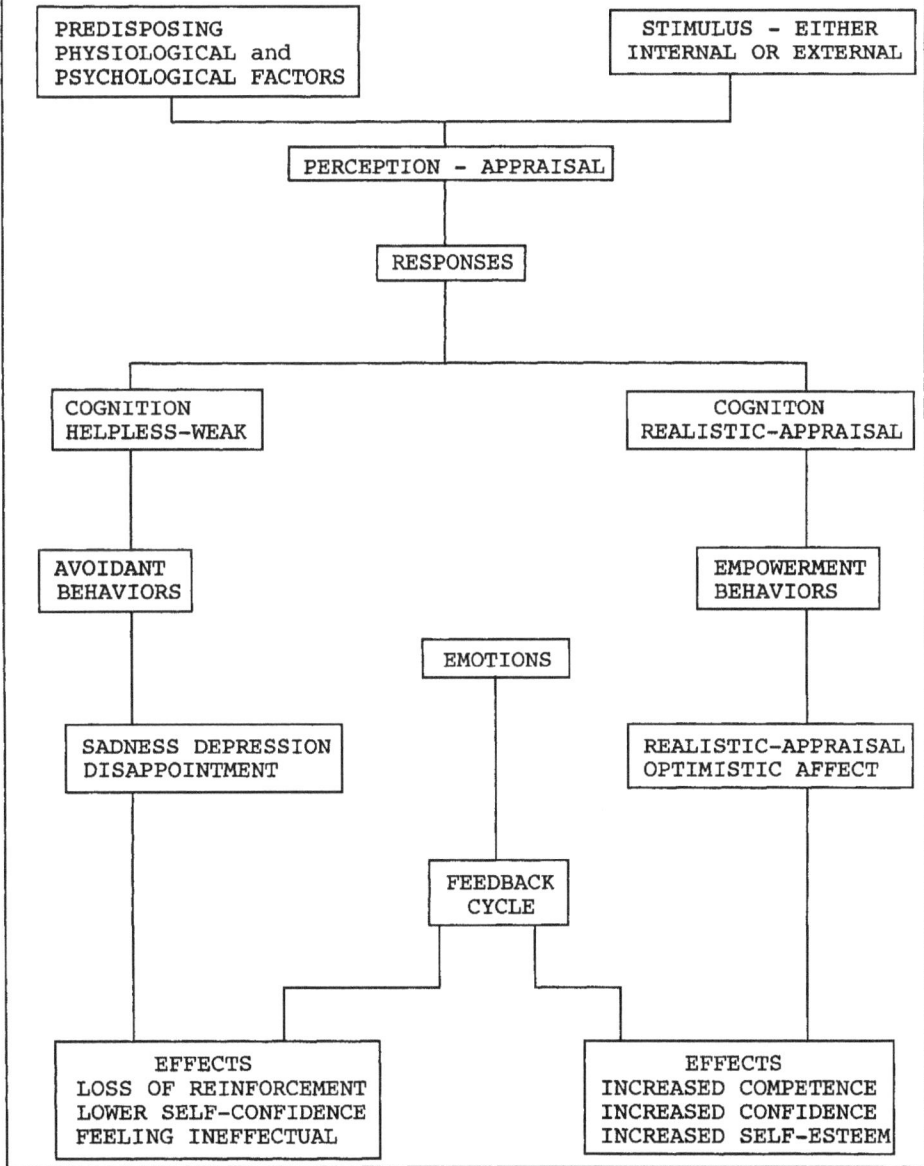

| PREDISPOSING PHYSIOLOGICAL and PSYCHOLOGICAL FACTORS | STIMULUS - EITHER INTERNAL OR EXTERNAL |

PERCEPTION - APPRAISAL

RESPONSES

| COGNITION HELPLESS-WEAK | COGNITON REALISTIC-APPRAISAL |

| AVOIDANT BEHAVIORS | EMPOWERMENT BEHAVIORS |

EMOTIONS

| SADNESS DEPRESSION DISAPPOINTMENT | REALISTIC-APPRAISAL OPTIMISTIC AFFECT |

FEEDBACK CYCLE

| EFFECTS LOSS OF REINFORCEMENT LOWER SELF-CONFIDENCE FEELING INEFFECTUAL | EFFECTS INCREASED COMPETENCE INCREASED CONFIDENCE INCREASED SELF-ESTEEM |

A COGNITIVE MODEL OF ANXIETY

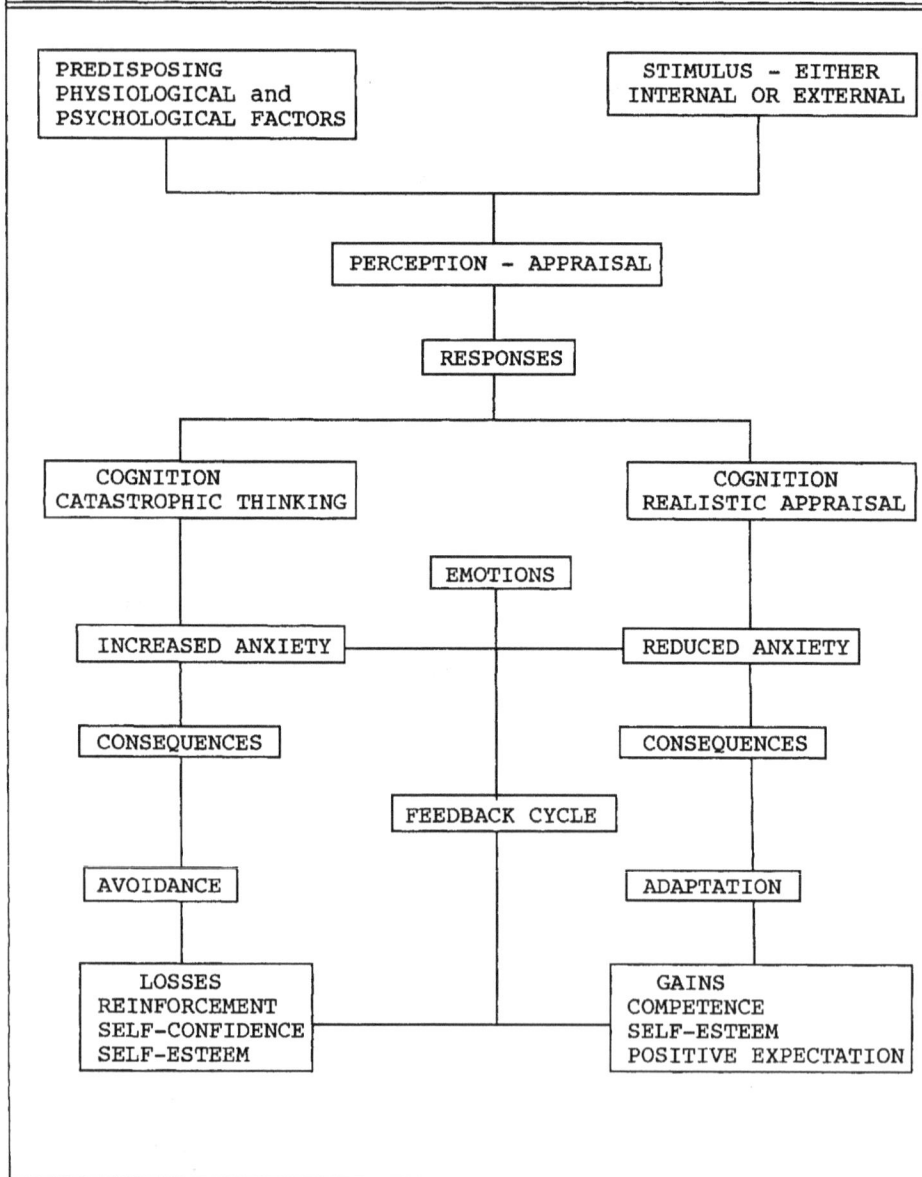

```
┌─────────────────────────┐              ┌─────────────────────────┐
│ PREDISPOSING            │              │ STIMULUS - EITHER       │
│ PHYSIOLOGICAL and       │              │ INTERNAL OR EXTERNAL    │
│ PSYCHOLOGICAL FACTORS   │              └─────────────────────────┘
└─────────────────────────┘

                  ┌─────────────────────────┐
                  │ PERCEPTION - APPRAISAL   │
                  └─────────────────────────┘

                  ┌─────────────────────────┐
                  │ RESPONSES               │
                  └─────────────────────────┘

┌─────────────────────────┐              ┌─────────────────────────┐
│ COGNITION               │              │ COGNITION               │
│ CATASTROPHIC THINKING   │              │ REALISTIC APPRAISAL     │
└─────────────────────────┘              └─────────────────────────┘

                  ┌─────────────┐
                  │ EMOTIONS    │
                  └─────────────┘

┌─────────────────────────┐              ┌─────────────────────────┐
│ INCREASED ANXIETY       │              │ REDUCED ANXIETY         │
└─────────────────────────┘              └─────────────────────────┘

┌─────────────────────────┐              ┌─────────────────────────┐
│ CONSEQUENCES            │              │ CONSEQUENCES            │
└─────────────────────────┘              └─────────────────────────┘

                  ┌─────────────────────────┐
                  │ FEEDBACK CYCLE          │
                  └─────────────────────────┘

┌─────────────────────────┐              ┌─────────────────────────┐
│ AVOIDANCE               │              │ ADAPTATION              │
└─────────────────────────┘              └─────────────────────────┘

┌─────────────────────────┐              ┌─────────────────────────┐
│ LOSSES                  │              │ GAINS                   │
│ REINFORCEMENT           │              │ COMPETENCE              │
│ SELF-CONFIDENCE         │              │ SELF-ESTEEM             │
│ SELF-ESTEEM             │              │ POSITIVE EXPECTATION    │
└─────────────────────────┘              └─────────────────────────┘
```

gentle, caring and competent dentist whom I had known for years. As I sought to understand the meaning of the "seemingly irrational," fear I made some important discoveries. The first was that lying on my back in a chair while I experienced the pain of someone working in my mouth I felt vulnerable, helpless and dependent. These are three very powerful triggers for anxiety, particularly if our psychological history has been problematic in these areas. And mine was! I had an abusive father who inflicted pain when I was dependent on him and helpless to do anything about it.

These very old unconscious feelings were triggered by an immediate environmental stimulus. This is often the way it works, anxiety can be a blend of old and present experiences. That is why it is very important to pay attention to the experience no matter how seemingly irrational or "without any real reason." Careful tracking of the experience can lead to important discoveries which will then make it possible to design appropriate coping strategies.

A third form of anxiety is one which has been receiving a lot of attention lately. **Panic attacks** are a severe form of anxiety characterized by its sudden onset, severity of symptoms and debilitating patterns of avoidance. Most people who have had a panic attack report almost uniformly that "It came out of the blue." Some even report that they were sleeping soundly and awoke terrified. This sudden onset is particularly disturbing because the symptoms occur in situations which have not previously caused any anxiety. People mistakenly, out of a need to explain the cause, attribute or associate the situation with the anxiety. They may be standing in line at the grocery store or the bank, or driving on the freeway when, suddenly, the anxiety begins. It then becomes associated with what they were doing. The symptoms are often so severe, because of the catastrophic expectations associated, that when they occur the person frequently seeks medical attention, Many who experience it think they are having a heart attack, may be going to die, lose control, go crazy or something else equally world ending.

Indeed, the mysterious onset, severity of the symptoms, and the associated physical sensations seem to be potentially lethal. The key here is *seems* to be. Since we all need to know what is going on and need to feel in control, this betrayal of the body is particularly terrifying. When a person discovers that by avoiding the freeway, bank, store, elevator, etc..., that the anxiety does not occur, it is a very natural tendency to seek control through avoidance. This secondary reaction of avoidance becomes a problem when anything which triggers anxiety serves as a new stimulus to anxiety. Hence, we now have a new phobia; fear of fear.

Anxiety, unlike depression, is easily generalized. This is a serious complication when one thing or another causes anxiety because the person begins avoiding more and more things. It may become so severe that the sufferer may be unable to get out of the house. For some, even the thought of becoming anxious triggers an attack. So a person becomes hyper—sensitized to any internal or external cue which has become associated with anxiety.

A variation of panic attacks which may occur with or without them is **Agoraphobia.** Agoraphobia is a fear of being in places or situations from which escape might be difficult or embarrassing. Closely related is a fear of not being able to get help, of being isolated, or alone. Common agoraphobic situations include being alone, traveling in a bus, plane, or car too far from home, being in crowds, or standing in lines. As mentioned previously, this problem has serious complications because as the person responds defensively, he/she often resorts to either avoidance or resorts to using chemicals to cope with anxiety.

The causes of anxiety, phobias, and panic attacks, like depression are varied. Again, the debate rages between those who advocate the physical causes and those who lean toward psycho-social causes. The overall profile of the anxiety prone person has several common features. The first commonality is usually an anxious childhood where one or both parents were fearful or there were situational variables which promoted insecurity; like divorce, family instability, alcoholism, or abuse.

The chicken or egg theory is problematic because if one is raised by anxious, unstable or alcoholic parents there is a strong likelihood of this creating problems for any child. A second common feature is a recent history of severe or prolonged stress. This appears to have an effect on the nervous system which causes a lowering of the anxiety threshold or sensitizes the nervous system by loading it up. Finally, there may be a loss of attachment or self-esteem which threatens a person's security. When these three factors are found together, there is a high probability of an anxiety attack.

Like depression, anxiety has special meaning for the individual. Regardless of whether there is a physical predisposition, anxiety has the function of signaling danger. Anxiety is experienced when something is perceived either internally or externally that triggers the body's alarm system. Once the emergency response system is activated, a very predictable physiological response occurs. The person is now activated to either fight or flee. The problem becomes acute when the danger signal is not known and appropriate coping responses cannot be found or are not known. The result is the very uncomfortable sensation of being in acute danger and not knowing what to do to escape the danger; in other words, by feeling helpless and out of control, the anxiety is fueled.

Coping with anxiety requires learning as much as possible. Because of the complexity, and various ways in which it affects each person differently, anxiety presents a challenge to both those who experience it and those who treat it. It has been found that a broad based approach which attacks anxiety on several fronts has the best chance of success. Just as in the case of depression, the starting place begins with *awareness*. It is particularly true in the case of anxiety that the more one can know about it the better one is able to cope. Knowing gives power and control over what was previously mysterious. Through *assessment* of the occurrence, the symptoms, the defenses and conditions which precede anxiety attacks certain patterns begins to emerge. Once these patterns begin to emerge the best line of attack will also emerge.

The first and most important thing to know about anxiety is that it is not lethal, nor does one go crazy from it. Even though it feels catastrophic, none of the things that are feared happen. Truly, the only thing to fear is anxiety itself. Therefore, education, frequent exposure, and reassurance are very important. A major factor in anxiety which tends to determine its course is *self-talk.* Once again, what determines our response is how we perceive the stimulus. Therefore, an important step in coping with anxiety is changing our thoughts about it. The first thought to change is its catastrophic nature. Do a reality check on the fears. What is the likelihood or probability of any of the feared consequences happening?

Reality checking the basis of fears leads to an important step. Listening to negative self—talk, this is a procedure to which we have referred several times. It is applicable again here. In this regard it is important to see how these feelings may be increased by negative self—talk. The most important thing is to develop awareness of the things which are told to oneself about the anxiety and one's ability to cope. Usually, the thoughts are undermining and devaluing of coping abilities. These thoughts need to be changed to realistic statements about the situation, the ability to cope and the probable outcome. These positive affirmations shut off the feelings of panic and helplessness which come from the perceived overwhelming nature of the catastrophe.

Besides awareness and cognitive modification, a third important coping technique is relaxation. Relaxation shuts off the emergency alarm system. One cannot be physically relaxed and anxious at the same time. It is impossible! Visualizing the feared situation while relaxed is a common form of systematic desensitization. It will help one to shut off the negative expectations and reduce the fear by de-conditioning it. Gradual self-exposure to feared objects and situations while relaxed is also another way to desensitize anxiety.

Finally, self-exploration in terms of one's early childhood experiences often leads to uncovering areas of vulnerability and the origination of many phobias and sources of anxiety. One measure of the strength of the self is the capacity to bear anxiety and depression. By increasing the overall ability to cope one gains self-confidence and self-esteem. This needs to be strongly rooted in knowledge of oneself.

In summary, anxiety may be dealt with by employing several strategies which encompass the cognitive, behavioral, and the emotional. Changing thoughts, negative self-talk, relaxation training, systematic desensitization, and self-understanding are all important to effectively cope with anxiety. Confronting avoidance by substituting more active and assertive behavior will increase self-esteem and decrease anxiety.

CHAPTER 7

DEPRESSION AND ANXIETY

EXERCISES

EXERCISE 1 DEPRESSION

Pick a very specific target that you think will reduce your depression by gaining mastery.

Why does it cause depression? What, realistically, can you do about it?

Make a specific contract with yourself about how you plan to deal with this problem.

Give yourself homework every day to work on this.

Keep a chart of how it affects your life.

Schedule activities with friends which are positive and reinforcing.

Visualize daily, yourself doing things which make you feel good about yourself. Do them!

EXERCISE 2 ANXIETY

Do a complete behavioral analysis of the things which make you the most anxious.

Chart what occurs before you become anxious.

Chart your thoughts about the anxiety.

Chart your responses —how did you cope— was it avoidance?

Now that you have learned everything about your anxiety, explore how long it has been a problem.

Are there areas of vulnerability which you can do something about?

Work out a strategy for systematically approaching and handling the problem.

In this plan include ways to handle the thoughts.

Practice relaxation techniques daily.

Setup a graduated plan for exposing yourself to the anxiety.

Keep working at it. It will go away.

Confront the fear rather than avoid it.

CHAPTER 7

DEPRESSION AND ANXIETY

EXERCISE 3

Develop secondary supportive skills. For example, if it is a fear of public speaking, take a class in communication.

Do not criticize yourself because you have the problem.

HOMEWORK SHEET

For one week, use this sheet to keep track of situations which produce anxiety or depression.

I

A. Situation
B. Emotion
C. Ideas — Self—talk
D. Consequences

II

A. Challenge the Ideas

1. Find the illogical idea

2. Is there any reality to it?

3. Why might the idea be false?

4. What is the worst that will happen?

5.   What good might happen?

6.   Are there other ways of looking at it?

What emotions and consequences might occur if you looked at
it differently?

CHAPTER 7

DEPRESSION AND ANXIETY

EXERCISE 4

RELAXATION AND DESENSITIZATION

In the section on stress you learned **Relaxation** and
Meditation techniques. These are excellent for dealing
with anxiety in two ways. (1) **Relaxation** produces
dominance of the pleasure response and (2) **Meditation** stops
the anxiety producing thoughts: a calm mind reduces anxiety.

Guidelines for using Relaxation and meditation for
desensitizing anxiety.

   (1) Practice 20 minutes a day using both progressive
        relaxation and meditation
   (2) Practice in a quiet place
   (3) Practice at regular times.
   (4) Practice using meditation to let go and detach from
        anxious thinking.

EXERCISE 5

COPING WITH A PANIC ATTACK

Panic attacks can be extremely distressing and lead to many
avoidance behaviors which can impact your lifestyle. The
following sequence is designed to help you develop confidence
and reduce the feelings of anxiety and helplessness
associated with loss of control.
If you experience panic:

   1. **Retreat** There is always an escape hatch. Take control
      i.e., leave the supermarket or get off the freeway.
      Retreat is different from avoidance. Avoidance is
      staying away from fearful situations. Retreat means
      leaving if uncomfortable beyond your tolerance and then
      returning.

2. **Distract** Panic and anxiety increase by focusing on the fear.

   A. Talk to someone about anything.

   B. Move around, engage in physical activity This discharges the adrenalin which is a result of the panic.

   C. Engage in repetitive mental activity—count cars, recite a poem from memory, count backward from 100 by subtracting 7. The list is endless—just redirect from how bad you are feeling to another activity requiring focused attention.

   D. Engage in an activity you find soothing. e.g., crossword puzzles, jig saw puzzles hobbies etc.

3. **Get Angry.** Anger and anxiety are incompatible reactions. Express it through yelling, pounding pillows, bags, tear up phone books. Vigorous exercise—smash tennis balls against a wall, chop wood, break ceramics. I have a client who models clay figures of people she is angry with and then pounds them.

4. **Turn on Pleasure.** Pleasure is also incompatible with anxiety.

   A. Prepare a snack or good meal use complex carbohydrates and protein. Avoid sugars and junk food and stimulants.

   B. Engage in sexual activity.

   C. Take a hot bath or shower.

5. **Thought Stopping.**

   A. Tell yourself Stop!
   B. Redirect thoughts.
   C. Meditate on positive scene Visualize it.
   D. Repeat your list of positive affirmations one at a time.

6. **Relax.** Use your deep muscle relaxation and controlled deep breathing. Slow down your breathing by taking long—slow—controlled breaths.

7. **Utilize.** Positive cognitive coping skills developed in chapter 4.

Pay attention to what works for you and use any combination you find helpful. Remember intense panic is short lived. You will not go crazy, lose control, or die. Practice these techniques regularly.

from The Anxiety and Phobia Workbook
        by Edmund Bourne.

NOTES

CHAPTER 7

ANXIETY AND DEPRESSION

FURTHER READING

Bourne, Edmund. The Anxiety and Phobia Workbook. Oakland, California; New Hurbinger Publications, 1990.

Burns, David. Feeling Good. New York: Signet, 1981.

Sheehan, David. The Anxiety Disease. New York: Bantam Books, 1986.

ANGER AND GRIEF

"My energy is coming back and it is scaring me. I had a dream in which a green monster with razor sharp teeth was eating me alive. I am so afraid I could hurt my kids, or I could hurt my wife or even myself, I am such a monster because of my anger,"
Alcoholic Middle-aged Methodist Minister

Anger is a powerful force in the lives of people. It contains the energy for self—preservation and great creativity and also the power to disrupt and destroy. It is present, always present, but often denied and unrecognized. In this chapter we will learn to recognize and become aware of anger, decipher it's complex messages and find constructive ways to give it expression.

Anger wears many masks. In its undisguised form it may be seen as full blown rage or an uncontrolled outburst. Anger is one thing in adults, another in an adolescent and still quite a different matter in a child. In its disguised form anger may come out as subtle satire, veiled sarcasm, irritability, vague hostility, or myriad forms of self-destructive and or anti-social behavior. Anger's many forms of expression range in intensity from mild to extreme and in appropriateness from the socially acceptable to blatantly destructive. Teaching people to deal with anger and to express it appropriately is a major function of society. Our first experience of anger usually begins with the family. It is in the commerce of every day living that children come to learn about anger's many complexities. Our experience of anger in this climate will determine, to a significant degree, how comfortable we are with our anger as well as the anger of others.

How well anger is handled in relationships, whether interpersonal or international determines, to a large extent, the success or failure of those relationships. Most societies have rituals and rules for managing conflict and redressing personal injury. War is one of those ritualized modes of aggression that governs international aggression.

Interpersonal war on a much smaller scale partakes of many of the same dynamics and has many of the same pervasive consequences to its victims.

Anger is a universal human experience. Everyone gets angry. It is as basic as all of the other human emotions we have been discussing. The problem with anger is that it is so threatening that some people have difficulty in recognizing it in themselves. Or in the opposite extreme, anger is so powerful that it is beyond control. The greater the difficulty in feeling, recognizing and controlling anger, the more difficulty a person will have in meaningful relationships.

We are born with the capacity for anger. It is necessary for our wellbeing. Anger, like all the other emotions, serves an important function in enabling us to survive in a complex world. The things which make us angry, the ways in which we respond when others are angry, and the particular feelings we have about our own anger are all learned. Our culture has very complex rules pertaining to anger; anger with children from adults; anger between adults who know each other; anger between adults who do not know each other; anger between male and female; the list is endless. These rules get transmitted through parents, peers, school, and the mass media.

Not all the rules about anger are necessarily helpful or even make sense. This is particularly true if one grew up in a dysfunctional family. In this kind of family the emotional climate may be far too controlled, or even entirely absent of feelings; in others, there may be too much of one kind of feeling and not enough of another.

What is characteristic of dysfunctional families is that not all feelings are permitted and feelings are judged as good or bad. In healthier families emotional output is consistent and appropriate. In this atmosphere, children know how their parents feel and why. It is especially easy to know when a parent is angry. This is because feelings —all kinds—are accepted. And what is most important is the child learns a feeling of comfort and safety from the expression of these feelings. People feel angry, or sad, glad, hurt, depressed, or tenderly loving. No one gets hurt, no one hurts themselves. People in this climate are what they feel; and it is acceptable. In this climate a child picks up the tone of consistency, openness, and warm acceptance regarding all feelings. The child learns: "I am loved and accepted; I am safe with my feelings; I don't need to stifle or pretend to please you." "I and all my feelings are welcomed in this family, I belong." Anger, then, is part and parcel of the ongoingness of people living together.

For many people, however, the emotional climate of their homes was not like this. So many have grown up afraid to feel, afraid to express feelings and afraid to be around others who feel and express their feelings. This is particularly true of anger.

In my particular family anger was strictly taboo. I learned that nice boys did not get angry. This taboo led to our family being cold and devoid of emotions. I never saw anyone express sadness, joy, or anger. The only anger, and it was destructive, was expressed by my father who ridiculed and demeaned my brother and myself for being weak, needy or tearful. What was communicated by this behavior was "don't feel, don't expose any weakness, and don't need; it is not safe to expose anything of yourself." The net effect is to deaden all feelings.

I remember being angry as a child, I had a very quick temper but soon learned to keep it hidden. The anger toward my father was suppressed: too dangerous to show. I became fearfully over-compliant. Occasionally I would "accidentally forget" to do something my father wanted me to do, or I would do something which drove him nuts. I was constantly getting my shoes wet. This, of course, drove him crazy, but how could he be mad at me? "I just forgot, or it was an accident." I was learning a process of denial, not taking responsibility for my anger and how to passively and indirectly act out my rage at him. *Take a moment here to*

212

write about how you express your anger. Feel free to
explore the rules for anger in your family. Do not
judge yourself for your feelings.

Anger which is not owned, felt, or expressed will be manifested somehow. It may turn inward in the form of guilty self—criticism or it may become totally repressed and thus experienced psychosomatically. These somatic expressions can take many forms. Headaches, ulcers, muscle tension, spastic colon, high blood pressure and allergic reactions are all common stress related disorders. It may also come out indirectly in other kinds of emotional reactions such as hostility, depression, anxiety, guilt, pouting, sullenness, irritability, and sudden rage.

There are many defensive strategies for dealing with anger, both our own and others. One defense against anger is *projection.* By attributing anger to others, it is safely disowned. As if to say this isn't my anger, everybody else is angry. Another is *displacement.* Kicking the dog is a classic example of displacing anger from the real target which may be dangerous to a target which is not as likely to retaliate. *Scapegoating* is another form of dealing with aggression indirectly. This is more often found in groups. Again, it is a means of dealing with anger which is felt within the group and taken out on a target outside the group. This defuses inner group tension and acts as a safety valve for feelings. These are just a few of the more common defenses found in dealing with anger and aggression. Though these defenses partially work to handle anger, they often do not get to the causes. Even more importantly, anger which is not handled constructively does not go awaay, it becomes a very contaminating, hidden force in all relationships.

The roots of anger are probably as numerous as there are people. However, there are several common causes which seem to transcend various cultures. Basically, anger is an innate biological and psychological reaction to threat, frustration or injury. It is part of the protective, defensive system which provides sufficient arousal to fight or problem solve. As was discussed in the segment on stress, emotional and central nervous system arousal may have many triggers, depending on the perception of the stimulus. These triggers are primarily learned and are a function of context and conditioning. The modes of expression or non—expression as the case may be, are also a product of prior experience.

In relationships where anger can be very threatening, it seems to arise out of dependency and interdependency conflicts. Most relationships have an instrumental function in that they are established to meet certain needs. These needs vary from economic to recreational to affectional. What is crucial to the welfare of these relationships is the degree to which conflict is managed. Anger is the byproduct of unmet needs and disappointed expectations. Hostility occurs because first of all, expectations are unclear to the person who has them, and secondly, they are not expressed to the partner. This leads to distance, retaliation: further complications.

A simple example comes to mind from a family that I have been working with. Problem: he was angry with her because she was not ready for church on time. Saturday night he had expressed an interest in going to church the next morning; she agreed. The next morning he got up and got ready. He became angrier and angrier as it got later and later. Finally, he stomped out and went by himself. Later he discussed it with me. Evidently, his wife decided that she couldn't go to church because she had too much to do around the house. Rather than tell him she had changed her mind, she merely got up and busied herself around the house and did the daughter's ironing and school clothes. She blamed the daughter for "having too much to do." He did not verbalize his anger to the wife, She did not tell him of her problem. The daughter was the scapegoat, she felt guilty, the wife was the martyr, and the husband became depressed.

This complex family interaction is illustrious of the many facets of anger. The first is in the history of the husband and wife. He was raised in a very dysfunctional home with an alcoholic father and mother who shamed and used guilt to control him. He learned very early to hide his anger and adopt an overly compliant, pleasing, caretaking, demeanor. The wife on the other hand, was raised by a mother who had violent chaotic relationships with several husbands; two of whom ended up being murdered. Her earliest memories are of hiding under the dining room table while plates and other objects smashed over her head.

Both individuals are fight phobic; in other words, fearful of anger and of confrontation. Each also has a great deal of difficulty in even recognizing their own anger.

215

In essence, anger is a complex emotion, which if it is not dealt with, can become a toxic force. A toxin which poisons the body, disrupts relationships, and results in many perverse psychological reactions.

Anger is complex because it has many sources. It may result from unmet psychological and physical needs, as well as stemming from beliefs, self—talk and expectations. It is paramount for our total wellbeing that we deal with our anger. The more that anger can be recognized, understood, and given direct expression the healthier individuals we will be.

Some signs of withheld anger include: an increase in anxiety, depression, and phobias, an increase in obsessive thinking, disturbances in sleep, and an increase in numerous self—destructive behaviors such as drinking, spending, eating or sexual escapades. At the somatic level, unexpressed anger may result in headaches, ulcers, spastic colon, high blood pressure, neck and back spasms, and chest pains. Clearly, an emotion this powerful needs to be dealt with consciously and responsibly.

Some guidelines for learning to come to grips with anger include: first of all, learn to recognize the signs of your own anger. Each of us, because of our histories, have a unique way of being angry. It is important to give yourself permission to be angry. It is normal for everyone to get angry. Include anger into your self—concept along with all of your other emotions.

Secondly, it is important to realistically appraise your anger. Many people are afraid that they will get out of control if they express it. The reality is that unexpressed anger is what leads to eruptions. This is because people repress their irritation and annoyance until it gets to explosive levels. If anger is dealt with immediately it seldom becomes a problem.

Thirdly, deal with any underlying fears you have about loss of love, losing people, or alienating them if you tell them what you want, need and feel. This is a dependency problem based on a need to please and have people like you so you can feel ok about yourself. Withholding feelings leads to greater complications. "We never fight," and "I am never angry" are both lies. Relationships based on these lies do not work.

Finally, it is possible to learn to express anger in ways which are non—aggressive, non—passive, and still preserve relationships as well as your self—esteem. Many of these techniques will be dealt with in the next chapter because they are critical for satisfying relationships.

If you find yourself unable to identify your anger or, if on the other hand, you function as a psychological terrorist and alienate everyone with your anger, you need a great deal of work in this area. When any emotion is excessive or lacking the solution is in discovering the attitudes, beliefs, and self—talk which may aggravate that emotion. Like all of the other emotions, anger is determined by our perceptions. People don't make you mad; you, relate to the situation angrily. This is the first hurdle in anger management, learning to take responsibility for your feelings

Learning to manage anger follows the same format as all of the other feelings. Step one is **awareness**. This can be done by returning to where you learned about anger; your family. You handle anger the way you were taught. It is important to recognize what the emotional climate of the home was and how emotions were expressed. Notice what makes you angry. **Accept** your feelings. What is going on inside of you and around you? Learn as much as you can by observing yourself being angry. Watch others when they are angry. See if you can discover hidden anger, (nice guys,) terrorists, (bullies), guerrilla fighters, (sneak attacks,) peace keepers, (placaters), victims, (those who let others abuse them) and addicts, (those who use their anger to get back at others).

Once you have raised your anger to a level of consciousness you are in a better position to deal with it by owning it and then choosing what to do about the things which anger you.

BEREAVEMENT—GRIEF

Bereavement is the actual experience of loss. Grief is our response to bereavement. I believe that the way we grieve is the defining process which, if understood, can tell us a great deal about healing and recovery. It is in our response to loss, our having to come to grips with death, our mortality, our vulnerability, painful emotions, confronting our beliefs about life, and how we go about comforting ourselves, we reveal our basic selves. In dealing with grief we use all of the skills we have been working on throughout this book. Let us look more closely at the grieving process.

Grief is experienced as a conflicting mass of emotion in reaction to a loss. The magnitude of the loss is determined by the significance of that which was lost. The loss may be anything to which we have an attachment; a relationship, house, job, parent, friend, child, or a significant life change in which some part of self is lost. In the latter, grief is a response to a natural life process in which we must go through changes. For example, retirement, college graduation, moving away from home, changing jobs, marriage and the children growing up and leaving home. Grief may also be experienced when an addiction is given up.

Grief, in essence, is an integral part of life and death, growth and decline. Grief is another of those very significant emotional experiences for which most of us are ill-equipped to cope. I remember my first experience with grief was when a close friend of mine in graduate school died very suddenly. I did not know how to respond to the feelings which threatened to overwhelm me. Sadness, numbness, emptiness, anger, confusion, and fear seemed to alternate in rapid succession. Since that time I have had other encounters with grief; the loss of a father and mother, death of a child, suicide of a close friend, the death of several distant relatives, and a divorce. Though grief is no longer a stranger it is still difficult to lose someone. Each loss is mourned in a different way. What is shared herein is a compilation of what I have learned in dealing with my own

219

grief as well as helping others with theirs. It is offered in the spirit of compassion for all of those who are grieving or have yet to recognize what may be a need to grieve.

First of all, grief can be a very lonely experience because what we lose is usually very personal to us. What is most difficult is to feel the depth of the loss while everyone else in the world seems to be going about their business as usual. People who grieve in our culture often grieve alone because others do not know how to respond effectively or comfortably. There are many taboos associated with death: strong emotion, revealing personal fears and inadequacies, and loss of control. These operate to keep people at a social distance. I as well as a number of clients have felt the social stigma of grief.

The discomfort of grief also causes people to communicate all the wrong things. For example: "It was for the best; you have to be strong; don't feel bad; they aren't really gone; they have gone to a better place; and time heals all wounds." Most of these responses communicate the unconscious messages of denial, avoidance, and repression of the very strong emotion of grief. As a result, people often turn off their emotions and grieve in isolation. They compound the problem by feeling guilty for not being able to get over the experience like "they should." This is called, secondary injury.

Grief is a process which seems to follow several steps. These steps are not always in the same order and are not accomplished in predictable amounts of time. But according to

Elizabeth Kubler—Ross, grief seems to involve the following stages. The first stage is **characterized by denial.**

STAGE ONE - DENIAL

"No, it can't be, it's not true," is the common response to news of a death or to the news of one's terminal illness. It takes time to incorporate the impact of the news. For many, denial is the first line of defense when it comes to dealing with any strong emotion. Usually, awareness dawns in small bits and bursts of emotion. Denial is a normal response to keeping oneself from being totally overwhelmed by something which potentially may be devastating. With denial comes the psychological numbing and shock. When a loss is felt to be "more than one can possibly bear", the natural defense is to not feel. Again, there is no formula which states that a person should only be in denial for 3 weeks or 6 months. It is up to the individual's capacity to bear the loss which determines how long it takes. The capacity to bear loss, of course depends on who or what the loss was, and other factors going on at the time. Also, a very significant factor is the amount of social support one has while grieving.

Stage Two - Anger

We feel anger because it hurts to lose something or someone. We also feel anger because we lose our cherished beliefs about life. Betrayal and abandonment are the most common responses to being left behind. These feelings, of course, engender strong feelings of anger. It is also typical to feel the unfairness of the loss. People commonly ask two questions in the face of traumatic loss: "Why?" and "Why me?"

These questions reflect some very basic assumptions which hold our world together. The first assumption we operate on is the illusory view of our personal immortality and that of the ones we love. When this illusion is shattered we feel a sense of outrage. "This shouldn't be happening to me!" A second closely held illusion is related to our illusion of immortality; we also believe in a just, fair, and orderly universe. Loss also shatters this illusion. When these illusions fail, we are left feeling bewildered, angry and frightened. Death is possible, chaos can happen, we are not Lords of our universe, after all. The injury to our narcissism is powerful, it touches the unconscious belief of the good child: "If I am good, then I deserve to be treated fairly and have only good things happen to me."

Losing a loved one or discovering our own mortality threatens our feelings of safety, security, justice and comfort. We protest, we are angry, but there is no where to go with our anger; it is here we are aware of our helplessness, vulnerability, and dependency. We shake our fists at the gods and the uncaring and seemingly unfeeling universe. We would seek redress for our grievances, but to whom do we go to lodge the protest? This period of anger may be a critical crossroad. Many end up in anger and bitterness like a box canyon. It becomes a final psychological resting place. Apparently unwilling to go on or go through the anger, it becomes a defense against life and further injury. We seemingly do not want to form new attachments because we will just be hurt again. It takes real work and growth to get through this period and rejoin the living. To be able to live in spite of death means accepting death and loss as part of life.

Stage Three - Bargaining

This is an attempt to simultaneously deny and accept what is happening. Again, this phase is an attempt to cope with the magnitude of the loss. In a way, it keeps the person from feeling overwhelmed while dealing with the reality of the pain. Bargaining is like a child trying to put off the inevitable bed time by wanting water, then a story, etc. "I'll be good, just don't let this happen to me" seems to be the plea. As one of my friends says, "I'll be a missionary to Beverly Hills, I'll eat fish, give up the prime rib and baked potatoes. I'll stop smoking and drinking. Just let me live!" When denial fails, the anger is spent, and the bargaining fails, we hit bottom.

Stage Four - Depression

Depression is the inevitable experience of the futility and emptiness of our loss. There is nothing to do. It has happened. We are left to deal with it as best we can. Being depressed is part of the recovery process. We try to defend against it, distract ourselves, cling to the lost person or life. We try frantically to fill the void and escape the terror of death. But finally, we are there, when we accept this then we begin to heal. Depression cannot be sidestepped in recovery. Paradoxically, facing depression leads to the final step, acceptance. And , again, I cannot emphasize too strongly, this process is not simple or orderly.

Stage Five - Acceptance

Acceptance leads to regaining life in spite of sorrow. Acceptance means we own the circumstances of our loss and our human condition. Grieving leads to being able to enjoy the memories without the pain. Acceptance leads to finding new meanings and creating new attachments. We can live without regret, remorse, or guilt when we find the solace of acceptance. Acceptance leads to having no unfinished business.

The grief-recovery process involves moving through various stages of grief at our own pace. It is <u>our</u> grief. The important attitude is one of **awareness and openness.** It is difficult to do, but it is important to let yourself experience it. It is also necessary to take responsibility for your own recovery. No one is going to do it for you. This will help you feel less angry and victimized. A part of taking responsibility is taking action. Recovery and healing is an active process. It is important to move toward rather than away from people. And finally, finding new meaning and new attachments requires trusting life again. This is a dynamic process of change. Part of the change process is disorganization and then reorganization. The process of disorganization is painful and hard to tolerate but it is essential to growth.

It is important to have a view of the whole process of grieving: it is like riding a carousel. You may ride the angry horse for a while, but you will also ride the horses of terror, despair, loneliness, exhilaration, calm and confusion.

The carousel will spin very rapidly at times and at others you will feel stuck on one horse. You may feel you will never get off the carousel. Whatever the horse, ride it with awareness and all the skill you can bring to bear. The rest must be left up to faith and trust. You will recover. And finally, remember that the final stages of grief are rebuilding a life that will be sustainable. There is a future!

WORKING THROUGH

There are many aspects of grief which have a traumatizing effect. The extent of the trauma depends on several factors, these have to do with how sudden the death was, who died, and how important that person was to us. There are also a number of personal factors which determine how we will cope with the loss. This has to do with our own psychological makeup, our own personal history with regard to how much previous trauma we have experienced, and finally the quality of our recovery environment. Working through involves a three step process. The first step is the *impact phase*. This is the stage where we actually experience the loss. If it is a death, we deal with all of the details, the funeral, and all of the things which actually go with coping with the actual event. We do not do any grieving in this stage. Usually, people are numb and so busy taking care of things and just getting through it that they don't have time to grieve. We use different skills during the impact phase.

The second phase of grieving is the *aftermath*. In the aftermath we are left with the residue of the loss. Just as a disaster has the smoking wreckage, so too, a loss leaves its distinct aftermath. Some refer to this period as the death imprint. This is a very critical period because it sets the tone and direction for our grieving. In the aftermath the reality of the loss begins to set in. This is where we begin to experience the emptiness and depression. This is where the impact of the loss begins to hit. We become aware of the significance of the loss. If it was a spouse, the griever is aware of the empty house, sleeping alone, the loss of companionship, the rituals and ceremonies of living with someone. What is lost is a whole way of life. This is the aftermath. It is common to feel estranged from life during this phase. You will notice others going about their happy lives, no one seems to care or be aware of your tragedy.

Anger, loneliness and depression begin to surface. How you respond to this critical period is crucial for recovery. Some respond by withdrawing, others throw themselves into frantic activity. Some turn off the pain with drugs and alcohol. Coping with these feelings in ways that lead to healing is the task of the third phase, *rebuilding*.

Rebuilding after a traumatic loss is a formidable task. While dealing with loss and the psychological impact of traumat ordinary reality also makes demands. I am reminded of a debriefing I did for the Pomona Girl Scout council after a bus crash in which several girls were killed and many more injured. The council director's biggest problem was coping with the overwhelming demands of the trauma while also trying to run an agency. She said "I've got shocked parents, hurt kids, traumatized staff, media camped in the parking lot and 50 programs that I need to keep going." In these circumstances there is often little time for healing as the press of reality inexorably urges us to take care of business.

In many ways it is easy to throw ourselves into normalizing activities, they can be so comforting. To feel in control and competent again; to restore order and not feel so vulnerable and frightened; these are the needs, this is the surcease offered by the daily rhythm of our lives. After all, it was shattered by an extraordinary event, why not heal by giving ourselves to the ordinary, mundane task of mowing the lawn and doing the laundry? If this helps, do it!

Healing depends on what was injured. We cannot know what to heal or how to go about it until we really understand the nature of the wound. The regimen for healing pneumonia is quite different than the one prescribed for ulcers. If we do not go about healing from trauma with awareness and intelligence, then all of our actions may not lead to healing. In effect we can be left with a wound that won't heal. In my own case in the aftermath of the death of my daughter, I employed my usual defenses. Hard work, repression of painful feelings, withdrawal from intimacy, intellectualized despair and spent money to feel powerful. These endeavors did not lead to healing.

What does lead to healing? I have found that several important ingredients need to be present. The first necessary ingredient is the quality of the recovery environment. It is very difficult to weather a crisis alone. A great deal of research indicates that those who recover the best are those who have access to caring and supportive relationships. If one does not have family or friends who can provide this level of support then it is important to find a good support group. Many times it is difficult for family to provide the support we need because they may also be struggling with the loss as well. That is why the death of a child is particularly so devastating. In my case, I was dealing with my own grief, while also being confronted by my wife's pain. And she also had the same problem.

The second necessary ingredient is a grief partner. This can be a sponsor, a friend, a therapist, a guru, a priest or a pastor, but it needs to be someone who has been there and can guide you through the wilderness. Again, grieving alone and trying to recover by yourself makes the process more difficult than it already is. The benefit of a support group and a guide is that they afford the opportunity to ventilate powerful feelings without criticism or judgement. They can correct our faulty ideas and self—criticism while also providing a safe network of relationships that have not been disrupted by the loss. In a group situation you also have the opportunity to see that you are not the only one who has suffered.

Finally, grieving takes time. During the healing process we must repair the damage to our self—esteem, deal with the impact of loss and trauma on our ideas about the world i.e., meaninglessness, suffering, and the why and why me questions. Processing all of the painful emotions is no easy task either. All that can be done here is to permit ourselves to feel whatever it is we feel. Not feeling and avoidance of grief only leads to a delayed grief reaction.

The rest of the grieving process has to do with learning to live in a post grief—post-trauma world. This means rebuilding, learning to trust, care and get reinvolved. For many people this is the most difficult phase. There is no time line on this phase. Much of it depends on your ability to comfort yourself, the quality of your relationships, and how well you rebuild your world. The most critical risk in grieving is to get stuck and remain a victim. When this occurs, the world remains a bleak place and the victim learns to view the world from a position of helplessness, despair and bitterness! The antidote to this position is self—empowerment. Again, we often can't control what happens to us, but we can control how we respond.

NOTES

CHAPTER 8

ANGER AND GRIEF

EXERCISE 1

ANGER AWARENESS

1. How was anger dealt with in your childhood home?

2. How did others respond to your anger?

3. What are your anger triggers?

4. How do you express your anger? To others? At yourself?

5. How do you feel after you have been really angry?

EXERCISE 2

DISCHARGING ANGER

Many times we find ourselves frustrated, irritable, or just angry and need to express it without hurting anyone.

Try a variety of techniques until you find an outlet that works for you. Remember, that this does not solve the problem, it is merely a way of letting off steam.

1. Write it out.

2. Shout it out. Find a place where no one can hear you and really express how you feel.

3. Pound a pillow.

4. Hit a tennis ball against a wall.

5. Tear up a phone book.

6. Play racquetball alone.

7. Hit a punching bag.

8. Use modeling clay and throw it against a wall.

9. Give yourself permission to feel the anger and vent it.

CHAPTER 8

ANGER AND GRIEF

EXERCISE 3

1. Sit quietly and focus your attention on a situation or a person which frequently creates anger in you.

2. Let yourself feel the anger. Give yourself permission to feel angry.

3. Notice the physical sensations associated with your anger. Learn to identify your anger with these sensations. Let them be without judgement.

4. Make a list of sentences which begin with the words: "I feel angry when...."

5. Analyze these sentences. Is there a common theme running through your anger?

6. Own your anger. Get a sense of the anger belonging to you. No one makes you angry. Your anger is a response to situations because of the way you are perceiving them. Try saying " I make me angry."

7. Take charge of your anger. Change the things which you feel angry about.

8. Develop an action plan for systematically taking control.

9. Empower yourself with the anger. Use it to motivate yourself to change.

10. Stop blaming and complaining. Take responsibility for your feelings.

CHAPTER 8

ANGER AND GRIEF

EXERCISE 4

1. Make a chronological time line from the time of your birth to the present day. Divide it into 5 year segments. In each segment write down any losses which caused you grief.

2. Note what memories and feelings you have about those losses. Have you completely dealt with them? You can tell by how you feel about them. Is there still a lot of pain, unresolved anger, regret? Note the one where you feel incomplete.

3. Make a list of regrets and unfinished business with the person you have lost. If it is a person write them a letter saying all the things you wished you had said.

4. Find a sponsor or someone you can be honest with and discuss your feelings of loss and grief. It helps to break out of your isolation by talking with someone.

5. Notice in your losses the attitudes you have about grieving and your feelings. It is important to let yourself have the feelings.

6. Notice where you are in the grief cycle. Are you denying? Clinging? Do you still hang on to things? Have you enshrined the person?

7. Try to say goodbye. Express your appreciation regret, and fond memories.

8. Move on. Reach out. Do some things to pleasure yourself. Start some new activities and routines with new people.

CHAPTER 8

ANGER AND GRIEF

EXERCISE 5

GRIEF MYTHS

Listed below are a number of myths based on erroneous ideas about grief. See which ones you may have fallen into which could complicate or prevent your grief resolution.

1. All bereaved people grieve the same way.

2. Grief declines over time in a steadily decreasing fashion.

3. When grief is resolved it never comes up again.

4. Family members will always help grievers.

5. Children grieve like adults.

6. Feeling sorry for yourself is not allowable.

7. It is better to put painful things out of your mind.

8. Do not think about your loss at Christmas because it will make you too sad.

9. Bereaved people only need to ventilate their feelings and they will resolve their grief.

10. Expressing feelings that are intense is the same as loosing control.

11. There is no reason to be angry at people who tried to do their best for the deceased.

12. There is no reason to be angry at the deceased.

13. Only sick individuals have physical problems in grief.

14. Because you feel crazy, you are going crazy.

15. You should only feel sadness that your loved one has died.

16. Miscarriage, neonatal loss, or sudden infant death shouldn't

be too difficult to resolve because the child was not known that well.

17. Children need to be protected from grief and death.

18. Rituals are unimportant to help us deal with life and death in contemporary America.

19. You should feel better knowing that there are other loved ones still alive.

20. There is something wrong if you do not always feel close to your spouse or other children, since you should be happy that they are still alive.

21. There is something sick about you if you think that part of you has died.

22. If someone has lost a spouse,they knows what it feels like to lose a child.

23. When in doubt about what to say to a bereaved parent, offer a cliche.

Note cliches others have used which hindered your grieving.

CHAPTER 8

ANGER AND GRIEF

FURTHER READING

Kubler—Ross. E. On Death and Dying. New York: Macmillan. 1969.

McKay, Mathew, Rogers, Peter, Mckay, Judith. When Anger Hurts. Oakland: New Harbinger Publications. 1989.

Parles. C. M. and Weiss, R. S. Recovery from Bereavement. New York: Basic Books, 1983.

Rando, Therese, A. ed. Parental Loss of a Child. Illinois: Research Press Co. 1986.

Rubin, I. R. The Angry Book. New York: Collier Books. 1969.

Travis, Carol. Anger: The Misunderstood Emotion. New York: Simon and Shuster, 1982.

NOTES

CHAPTER 9

RELATIONSHIPS

To love means to be actively cconcerned for the life and growth of another. One must be responsive to the needs (physical and psychic) of the other. One must respecxt the uniqueness of the other, to see him as he is and to help him grow and unfold in his own ways, for his own sake and not for the purpose of serving oneself. But one cannot fully respect the other without knowing that other deeply.
Irvin D. Yalom

The essence of relationships—togetherness, separateness and loving nurturance, are the foundation of human identity. For it is in precisely the dynamic ambivalence of relationships that we experience our greatest fears, deepest needs, most private agonies, greatest confusion and ultimate fulfillment. Being known, accepted, understood, and affirmed for our very selves becomes the basis, the foundation of our own self—knowledge, understanding, acceptance, self—affirmation, and ultimately self—actualization.

In previous segments we have discussed the importance of relationships to self—identity. It is impossible to write of or to discuss human problems and development without having a look at the context in which all of this occurs. We are at every moment in relationship. Relationship is the very nature of being. Whether it is physical, social, interpersonal or to our self, a relationship is our very way of being in the world. It is the quality and characteristics of our being in

237

the world which defines us (our modus operandi). In other words, who we are comes to be defined by our relational style. With this in mind, let us examine more closely some of those qualities of relationships which are so defining of our identity.

We will begin by looking at how the poet Kahlil Gibran expressed his view of love and relationships. Sometimes poetry expresses more richly the complexities and nuances of the heart than all of the psychology textbooks combined.

> *Then Almitra spoke again and said,*
>   *And what of marriage, Master?*
> *And he answered her saying:*
> *You were born together, and together*
> *you shall be forever more.*
> *You shall be—together when the*
> *white wings of death scatter your days and*
> *you shall be together in the*
> *Silent memory of God.*
> *But let there be space in your*
> *togetherness.*
> *And let the winds of heaven*
> *dance between you.*
> *Love one another, but make not*
> *a bond of love.*
> *Let it be rather a moving sea*
> *between the shores of your souls.*
> *Fill each other's cups*
> *but drink not from one cup*
> *Give one another of your bread*
> *but eat not from the same loaf.*
> *Sing and dance together and be*
> *joyous, but let each of you be alone*
> *Even as the strings of the lute are alone*
> *even though they quiver with the same music*
> *Give your hearts but not*
> *into each other's keeping*
> *For only the hand of life can contain*
> *your hearts*
> *And stand together yet not*
> *too near together.*
> *For the pillars of the temple stand apart*
> *And the oak tree and the cypress*
> *grow not in each others shadow.*
>   Kahlil Gibran THE PROPHET

Gibran notes the essential paradox in our being together. He suggests that there be space in our togetherness. How to be separate is one of the more difficult aspects of relationships. This is one of those chicken—or—egg quandaries. Which comes first, togetherness or separateness? Can you have one without the other? I believe separateness is essential to the success of any relationship. But the ability to be separate is dependent upon our having had good experiences with togetherness. Separateness is the ability to stand alone, to be self—dependent. In psychological terms, we call this *Individuation.* Individuation is the process by which a child becomes aware of being a self that is separate from others and has developed the ability to be self—sufficient. An individual with self—identity has an adequate self—image, positive self—esteem, clear boundaries, is competent in managing the affairs of life, and is self—nurturing. All of these ideas express the qualities of being separate as a person. Being separate does not mean not needing anyone or not caring about others as so many people seem to think. Individuation is not selfishness.

Being able to function autonomously in the world as an individual also means having the same kind of competence in relationships. The two are inter—dependent. Being intimate with another person implies closeness without losing one's self—boundaries (identity) and not needing to take over the other person's identity (fusion). Many people mistake the feeling of closeness as merging with another or fusing their ego with someone else's. This is the problem of co—dependency. Co—dependency is the opposite of individuation. People who need to feel fused with another or need to rescue or somehow make a career of feeling responsible for others have not individuated. In order to function independently in relationships, one must have secure boundaries and trust: trust in oneself and trust in the other. Trust is the cornerstone of all relationships.

Separateness implies the ability to stand alone; to tolerate both intimacy and distance, simultaneously. It means tolerating your partner's dependency and independence, as well as your own. Being comfortable with neediness in yourself and others suggests that you are capable of self—nurturance. You feed each other but not from the same loaf; this suggests the ability to give from within, that you are bringing something into the relationship and that you are not feeding off each other in a symbiotic or parasitic way.

Lack of individuation presents itself in many ways. People who have difficulty in this area usually are low in self—esteem, are passive and dependent, fear being alone, lack self—confidence, are fearfully jealous, have difficulty expressing anger and have strong needs to please others. This constellation of problems often leads to victimization or abuse in relationships. One cannot be intimate if one has never learned to be separate.

Intimacy is defined as the experience of closeness. Mutuality and openness are created by two persons who are strong enough to be vulnerable and trusting enough to be without defenses. In short, who are whole enough to love and be loved without needing the other to make them whole.

The impact of unresolved dependency problems (failure to individuate) on a relationship is considerable. When a person who feels incomplete in his/her own personhood gets into a relationship he/she unconsciously is looking for completion. This hidden agenda has to do with the expectation that "When I find someone to love me and take care of me, then I will be okay." The expectation is that the other person is supposed to take care of me, make me feel good, make me feel like a real person and through identification with him/her feel like I am somebody. These hidden expectations frequently end in disappointment and disillusionment. The old refrain, "I don't know what happened. He/she changed. We stopped loving each other, we grew away from each other, etc." reflects the outcome of this process.

The need for love is normal, the need for intimacy is normal, wanting to be with someone is normal. Seeking gratification of our dependency needs under the guise of love is where the problem arises. In being together, trying to get our needs met and meeting the other person's needs as well, requires a high level of maturity.

The legacy of dysfunctional families is considerable in the kinds of difficulties their children have in establishing and sustaining meaningful relationships. For example, I have a client, a 24—year—old man who was raised in a family where the father was a hard—working alcoholic. Mother was anxious and depressed. She turned her anger at her husband inward and in her loneliness turned to her young son for companionship and love. She did everything for him; she lavished all of her attention and her love on this child who returned her love. They developed a very special bond. Though he had his mother's love, he also needed a father. Father was never home. When he was, it was a disaster. My client's worst memory was one Christmas when his father came home drunk and knocked over the Christmas tree. Christmas day he was sick with a hangover and yelled at everyone.

When it came time for my client to leave home for college, he couldn't. He became so tormented with guilt and anxiety that he fell apart and ended up in a psychiatric hospital. At the core of his conflict was the feeling of responsibility for his mother. "If I leave her she might die or she might kill herself and it would be all my fault." On the other side of the conflict, he was so angry that he was terrified by his thoughts of killing her. The classic dependency bind. I can't live with you and I can't live without you.

There are several areas of obvious dysfunction in this family which I'd like to comment on because it so clearly illustrates the essentials of relationships. These areas —Roles, Boundaries, Nurturance, and Communication—are illustrative by their poor quality in this family. They do, however, when working well, form an interrelated matrix that provides the necessary and sufficient conditions; the very foundation of a healthy human personality and healthy family.

Roles, the ways in which we fulfill our various tasks in life, refer to our gender identity. This is a difficult problem to discuss in today's climate because of the problem of sexism and sex—role stereotyping. I am using the term to indicate the ways in which our society has taught us to behave toward each other as men and women. Historically, these roles were more clearly distinct than they are now. Simply put, in the case of my client, he did not grow up knowing how to be an independent man. Mother's involvement and father's absence led to his psychologically remaining a little boy. He over—identified with his mother. From her he learned to be sensitive, caring, giving and concerned for others. From his father he did not learn independence, aggression, competitiveness, self—responsibility, industry or how to relate to other men. These masculine and feminine principles were not integrated in this family. It is necessary in our world to integrate these qualities. In fact, the term androgyny is being used today to describe a person who embodies the qualities of sensitivity, strength, nurturance, independence and empathy. Androgyny has been found to be necessary for healthy relationships in our kind of society, (this is true for both men and women). In order for men and women to comfortably and successfully relate to each other, each must be integrated within themselves with regard to their masculine and feminine features.

Many failures in relationships are due to men who are not good at nurturing and women who have not found their own strength. The problem of sex role expectations and sex role identity begins in child rearing practices. Little girls have traditionally been taught to be nice, cute, dependent and to

243

look for their identity in attracting a "strong man". Little boys are taught to be competitive, aggressive, unfeeling and most of all, to not cry. Men are taught to value women as sexual objects. These inadequate sex role expectations lead to severe relationship difficulties. Men who relate to women as sexual objects or "mother figures", soon grow restless and bored or become trapped by what they project as mothering by their mates. Women become disillusioned and frustrated by not getting their needs for companionship and sensitivity met. The inevitable failure of these dysfunctional ideas are responsible, in large measure, for such a high divorce rate.

The lack of role integration and clarity leads to confusion in the children. In the case of my client, he finds himself not knowing how to be independent and assertive. He is attracted to women who are depressed and need him to take care of them. He has difficulty in asserting his own needs and verbalizing his frustration. Consequently, he stifles his anger for fear of rejection and abandonment. He tends to be intense and over—involved. He spends little time on his own projects, preferring to spend all of his time with her. This leads to his partner feeling suffocated, so she withdraws. He feels this and becomes anxious. He feels as if he must have done something wrong. This continuous cycle of dependency conflict illustrates lack of individuation.

Resolution of dependency conflicts, integration of sex roles and achieving individuation requires serious work. We must come to understand the ways in which it has influenced us, heal the wounds from the toxic aspects of parenting and free ourselves from the chains of habitual ways of relating. What was modeled by the parental relationship becomes a learned pattern of behavior which is carried forward in an internalized form as a self relationship. In other words, I treat myself the way my father and mother treated me, and I relate to others the way they related to each other. It becomes a tired old rerun of an ancient drama that is relived time and time again. History repeats itself over and over. Have you noticed that your relationships seem to follow the same pattern as those of your parents? Have you noticed yourself relating to your own children the way your parents related to you? This destructive cycle can be interrupted if we are willing to learn new ways of relating to ourselves and others. Dealing with our feelings about mother and father can lead to a resolution of those old conflicts, lead to an acceptance of them, and enable us to go on in a new way, free from anger, guilt and regret. In order to do this we need good bouindaries.

Boundaries, like fences, make good neighbors. As mentioned previously, it is essential to a good relationship for both individuals to have strong self-identities—to have progressed well along in their quest for autonomy. This means that a person who is growing toward independence is not seeking completion of their missing self in the other. A separate person takes responsibility for meeting their own needs, and solving their own problems. Quite frequently, problems arise because of poorly established boundaries in which there is an unconscious wish for fusion. As if—you should magically know

245

my needs without my having to speak them and then act benevolently to gratify my every need. I have had clients say on numerous occasions, "If he/she really loved me, I wouldn't have to tell him/her what I want." This is a manifestation of poor boundaries. The person has not developed emotionally beyond the infantile—magical stage when the expectation is that the good mother or father is so tuned into the child that the child is made comfortable without having to do anything.

Having good boundaries, to summarize, means having a strong sense of our own identity. It means actively pursuing our own needs, being responsible for our own self—esteem, and being assertive in communicating these to our partners.

Boundary problems most often lead to feeling victimized and coerced in relationships. The victim is one who "never gets what he wants" Victims feel imposed upon and blame others for their condition. "You did this to me and it's not my fault" are classic victim statements. Victims have no sense of their own power in relationships. This powerlessness and helplessness is a result of the person feeling coerced because of dependency on the other person. Out of insecurity and the need to be loved, power is given over to the other. The result is being unable to say "no", to assert our own needs and to do what we need to do to feel good ourselves. It is common for people to mistake having good boundaries with selfishness. "I feel guilty when I do what I want to do, or when I say no to what someone else wants me to do." Establishing good boundaries requires being assertive.

Assertiveness presumes one has the right to exist and that

one's needs are as important as any one else's. An assertive boundary position is: "I have these needs; I would like them met. If we can get together, that would be very nice. You are free to meet my need or not. You are also free to put your needs into the arena, as well. I take responsibility for my needs; you do the same. You tell me what you need and I will do the same.."

Establishing boundaries reflects a healthy process in which two individuals enhance and compliment their individuality through the relationship. Neither expects the relationship to make him/her complete.

I went to a friend's wedding some time ago. During the ceremony the minister had the bride and groom light two candles. Then they lit a third from their own candles. Then he had them extinguish their own candles, leaving the third one burning to symbolize the unification of their lives. To me, the symbolism would be more powerful if he had let them keep their own candles burning. The difficulty I have with sacrificing individuality to the relationship reflects my years of experience in counseling couples. They get married with the idea of becoming one. But then they argue about which one. In short, I think that boundary problems can be averted by "letting there be space in our togetherness" and by continuing to work toward individuation through interdependence rather than dependence. The relationship can then take on the quality of each person continuing their struggle for self—actualization. And then in the process, nurturing each other, but not from the same loaf. This creates an intimacy that is much different than the false closeness of fused dependency.

Intimacy, the capacity for gratification from contact with another person, reveals a great deal about what our personal history with others has been. For it is in intimacy that old wounds are often exposed and hidden vulnerability is revealed. The way that we respond to the threat and power of intimacy determines the outcome of the relationship. Intimacy requires having come to grips with dependency issues, integrated our sex roles and established good boundaries. In short, true intimacy is only possible for those in the process of achieving psychological individuation. For those struggling in this area, we see a number of problems being manifested in a multi—determined way. Low self—esteem, dependency, role conflict, insecurity, anxiety, depression, psychosomatic illnesses and sexual difficulties contribute to or are part of the causal picture. Of course, these have their roots in early childhood learning experiences in the family. As I have said previously, the parent—child relationship is a paradigm for all future relationships.

It is this original encounter where the basis for intimacy is established. If this primal encounter is characterized by warmth, acceptance, and consistency, and if our dependency and vulnerability are safeguarded and our individuality cherished and nurtured, then we will develop a sense of basic trust in relationships. In essence, if we felt loved by those to whom we were entrusted in our infancy, then we will be capable of entrusting ourselves as adults in loving relationships. This is what I mean by our early attachments serving as our relational paradigm, our love blueprint.

But what is love? We have so many romantic notions about it that it is difficult to know what is meant when the word is used. Love at one and the same time expresses the trivial and the sublime. We use the same word in saying, "I love pizza, the Dodgers, America, God, and Mozart." What, then. are the essential qualities in loving that make for enduring relationships?

The cornerstone of loving is *TRUST*. Without trust, we do not make commitments. Commitment seems to frighten many people. For example, I have a client who has a real problem with it. His fear is "If I make a commitment, maybe I'll make a mistake. Maybe it won't work. Maybe she'll change. I don't want any ties that bind."

Difficulty in committing leaves him vacillating between lonely isolation on one hand and the opposite extreme of feeling encumbered and coerced by another's needs. Lonely or trapped—this either—or position keeps him perpetually uninvolved in life. It isn't just an intimate relationship he fears; he finds commitment to anything difficult. Basically, at the root of fear of commitment is the unresolved fear of dependency. As if, "I make a commitment to you, I might lose my independence or, even worse, I might need you, and then you might betray or abandon me." The lack of trust manifests itself as a lack of trust in not only oneself, but also in the basic trustworthiness of the other. It is a fear of being needed as well as needing and of course, betrayal and abandonment. With these powerful fears operating at the root of our personalities, it leaves us in a tremendous conflict: the need to be loved and the need to preserve our basic security and independence.

A second essential quality in loving is **RESPECT**. When we respect another, we value their individuality and put their welfare on a par with our own. To really respect another is to accept them for who they are and let them be. Respect means to not try and control, manipulate, or exploit the other. Again, respect begins with the ability to respect oneself which comes from having been respected as a child.

Closely allied with respect is the quality of *Caring.* To care for another is to actively strive to promote their well—being. Caring is nurturing and cultivating the growth of a person and the relationship. This presupposes that one places a high value on the other person and the relationship. Nurturing takes time and involvement. The perfect analogy for caring is growing things. To care for one's garden, one must cultivate, prune, water, feed, plant and actively safeguard from pests and predators. Then one waits for the fruit of the involvement.

Finally, a quality essential for all relationships is *Compassion.* Carl Rogers, a founding father of humanistic psychology, studied the qualities of healing relationships his whole life. For him, the necessary and sufficient quality for healing relationships was what he called "unconditional positive regard." This rather cumbersome technical term can be translated, I believe, into the term *Compassion.* Rogers found that when people—primarily young children—were subjected to conditions of worth (that is, their self-esteem was based on pleasing their parents) it had damaging consequences. Being good and fearing loss of parental love for making mistakes leads to perfectionism—the feeling that one can only be accepted if they are perfect.

Roger's primary concern in his research was the importance of being loved and accepted unconditionally for who one is, not what we do. If a child is afraid of rejection or is subjected to continual criticism these attitudes are internalized and the child becomes self-critical, judgmental and devaluing whenever a mistake is made. I was working with a client just the other day on this issue. She was totally unaware of how angry, critical and self-rejecting she was every time she made a mistake. Her expectations of herself were extreme and she had little tolerance for herself when she did not meet these expectations. When disappointed, she would become very depressed and self-castigating; merciless in her criticism. We have been working on developing a more compassionate attitude toward herself.

Compassion means, to me, that I know I am accepted by the other, that I can be deeply and openly myself without fear of rejection, criticism or ridicule. I know in this relationship that my humanity (warts, wrinkles, errors, faults and all) will be tolerated and forgiven. Without this confidence there can be no risk-taking, no self-disclosure. Without the assurance of compassion it is not possible to let the other really know me in the inner, secret, self. It is in this type of self-revelation when we are letting ourselves be known in our inner sanctum that the highest level of intimacy is achieved. Compassion leads to letting down the defensive armor which frees the spirit to grow, the horizons to expand. We feel free to pursue dreams, to experiment, to fail and hurt without the crippling and inhibiting judgement of conditional acceptance. And of course, it goes without saying that before we can have compassion for another we must have it for ourselves.

I am sure we have all felt how devastating it can be to reveal a dream or a secret fantasy and have someone laugh or ridicule us. I remember still my father's scorn when I cried over being told we were going to move and I would have to leave all my friends. His ridicule still rings in my ears when I think of the times I revealed my secret desires for a sports car. Could this explain my obsession with them as an adult?

Commitment, caring and compassion are fundamental qualities to intimacy. However, they need to be communicated. Failure to communicate leads to conflict and chronically unsolved problems which fester as lingering resentment. This creates inevitable distance and becomes a barrier to intimacy. Not only is it important to communicate, but it is also important how we do it. In any well functioning relationship, there is the necessity for communication of feelings, desires and appreciation as well as day-to-day information. These must be communicated, but how?

Some basic principles can make for success. First, the

communicator or sender of the message must take responsibility for the message. Own it. Messages work best if they are in the first person. "I feel hurt" is a better message than "you hurt me." The message reports my feelings. "I am hurt ." "I am confused." "I am bothered." All of these communicate the idea that I own the problem and am taking responsibility for my feelings. You messages are often perceived as critical, attacking, and blaming. These result in defensiveness which usually escalates into hostilities. "You hurt me because you are an irresponsible idiot!" leaves nowhere to go but anger. Obviously, this causes communication to go downhill fast. It certainly does not lead to problem-solving or good will.

A second important principle to keep in mind is to report feelings and give accurate information when communicating. Blaming and evaluative labels need to be avoided. Example: "Johnny, when you hit your sister, it hurts her and I don't like it." Labels tend to hurt and become part of self-image. When name-calling and character assassination occurs, it creates resentment, feelings of shame, guilt, embarrassment and lingering hurt. It closes off communication and causes avoidance, lying, and often becomes modeled (the child copies it as a form of self-communication).

Thirdly, communication cannot take place without active listening. Learn to listen with your eyes as well as your ears. Look at the person when you are trying to communicate. What is their body language communicating? Is it the same as their verbal message? Does the message match up with the emotional tone of their words? By listening for what is unspoken, for the subtle emotional tones as well as the overt message, one gets a more complete communication. Put yourself in the other person's place when listening. Empathy enhances listening.

The next step in active listening is to give accurate feedback of what is heard. This may be done with simple reflective statements: "You seem upset." "You seem very agitated." "You seem tired." Or you may give responses that communicate the apparent discrepancy in the message you are receiving: "I know you said nothing is bothering you, but you have been slamming doors, throwing dishes, and yelling at the kids. Perhaps you are more upset than you realize." By giving descriptive, accurate feedback, you are creating an atmosphere of active concern and keeping the process alive, this is the essence of dialogue. It is also an important part of the feedback process to realize that the message you heard may not be the message which was intended.

Communication is a very subjective process. We hear, we filter messages, we distort, we interpret what is being said through the screen of our emotional state at the time. Simple statements such as "What I heard you say was...." let you take responsibility for possibly misunderstanding the message. They indicate that you are seeking to really understand what is being said. It is very affirming to have someone actively listen, empathize, interact and understand what we are trying to say. People have said to me on many occasions, "You know, this is the first time someone has taken the time to really listen to me." And by having someone listen to us, we also may hear at a deeper level what we are saying and feeling.

Actively listening, accurate messages, feedback, and taking responsibility set the stage for one of the more difficult dimensions in relationships. Conflict resolution. Every couple fights, conflict is inevitable between people living together. There are hundreds of books on fighting; one of my favorites is " The Intimate Enemy." In this book George Bach emphasizes that passion is kept alive by effective fighting; dirty fighting creates distance and is the enemy of intimacy.

The essence of healthy fighting is stating clearly what the problem is and requesting change. This is hard for most people to do. Often we are not clear as to what the problem is and secondly most of the time we are sure the problem is our partner. It's not me—it's you! Another aspect of healthy fighting is directly saying what we are feeling. Since most people are fight phobic, this directness can be frightening. Saying what we want and need also involves a rather high level of self—esteem and freedom from shame. Saying what we want and need openly exposes us.

Requesting change is based on accurately formulating the problem and presenting a solution. This is the foundational principle in Assertiveness Training. This in brief, is a way of defining your terms for the relationship and putting them on the table. The next step is negotiation. This can be a very healthy process when each partner gets clear about expectations, preferences, wants and needs. At the infantile level we all want what we want when we want it. It is basic narcissism to want our way all the time. However, perhaps you have noticed that the world does not always revolve around meeting your needs exactly as you want them met.

Getting others to meet our needs and being able to meet their needs on a give and take basis leads to a win—win condition. If we feel that we lose more often than we win we will be resentful.

In one couple I work with, they formulated the problem this way: each felt they won 20% of the time and lost 80% of the time. This is a classic lose—lose relationship. It occurred because they both felt victimized and weren't dealing with it clearly and directly.

Owning the message, sending accurate messages, giving feedback, actively listening and requesting change are all techniques which improve communication. These simple ideas go a long way toward smoothing out the rough edges in relationships. They form the bridge to intimacy. Words and feelings withheld become cracks which may widen to uncrossable canyons in relationships over the years. Problems that go unsolved become barriers to intimacy. The enemy of intimacy is festering resentment, hurt that lingers and goes unhealed. The affront which is unforgiven becomes a hammer with which we hit back at the least insult.

Distance in relationships that doesn't get crossed becomes a barren field in the garden of relationships. We lose respect, we gather hurts, we begin to avoid and then we withdraw our love. After a while, we wonder what happened to the magic. What happened to all of those good feelings we used to have? Relationships must be actively nourished. Love cannot be taken for granted. Our appreciation and love must be communicated daily. It takes work to change relationships which have become angry and unsatisfactory. It takes both partners to make a commitment for change. It often takes a long time to regain trust because of hurts and resentments that have built up over the years.

Quite often, when a problem is initially addressed in therapy and brought out in the open, the relationship deteriorates because the couple has been hiding information. To bring it out in the open can be painful and lead to a time of confusion and discomfort. But at least it creates the opportunity for regaining an honest foundation for the relationship. Speaking the truth is the only way to resuscitate what may be a dead or critically wounded relationship.

Love one another, but make not a bond of love—

And let the winds of heaven dance between you.

CHAPTER 9

RELATIONSHIPS

EXERCISE 1

INDIVIDUATION

1. Set aside one hour when you can be entirely alone without interruptions. Sit quietly, no radio, no television, no distractions of any kind. Pay attention to what you are experiencing, what does it feel like to be with yourself? What is going on in your body? What are you thinking? Do you know how to be with yourself? Do you know how to be alone? If certain kinds of feelings or images come to mind, write them down, follow them up. Get to know yourself.

2. Go to a movie by yourself.

3. Go to dinner by yourself. Focus during the meal on the pleasures of eating and being served. Taste the food. What do you like to eat?

4. Plan a whole day to spend by yourself. A drive in the mountains? A day at the beach? Shopping? What do you really like to do? Do it.

5. Plan a project. Carry it out from beginning to end. Just do it and experience the feeling of completion and satisfaction, of being in control. Notice what kinds of resistance you might run into. Do you sabotage yourself from getting good feelings about completing tasks?

6. Give yourself a present. Do you have trouble giving to yourself? Guilt? Feel like you don't deserve it?

7. Spend a day being totally selfish. Think only of yourself. Put yourself first? What does this feel like? Would you want to do this all the time?

8. Give yourself one night out a week, entirely free from any responsibility. Is this hard for you to do? Is it hard for those around you to let you do?

9. Go play. Let yourself be a playful child. Can you be spontaneous?

Now that you have had some practice doing your own thing, where would you rate yourself on the individuation scale?

Dependent	Independent	Interdependent
Child	Adolescent	Adult

NOTES

CHAPTER 9

RELATIONSHIPS

EXERCISE 2

BOUNDARIES

How you interact with others can be a source of considerable stress. You may learn to reduce that stress by having good boundaries and communicating your needs clearly. Assertiveness training has been found to be effective for both these problems. Below are a few exercises in assertiveness which may help you clarify your interpersonal style and learn to communicate more effectively.

The first step in assertiveness training is learning to distinguish between three different styles of relating: **Aggressive**, **Passive**, and **Assertive**.

Aggressive: Examples of aggressive style: Fighting, accusing, threatening, demanding, and in general stepping on people without regard for their feelings.

Passive: A person is behaving passively when he/she lets others push them around without regard for how he/she feels about it. Generally, it is a failure to have good boundaries and stand up for who one is. Passivity has been learned to avoid confrontation and prevent rejection. The cost of passivity is feeling victimized, and a heavy burden of resentment, guilt, and anger is stored up.

Assertiveness: A person is behaving assertively when he/she stands up for his/her rights, expresses feelings directly and does not permit others to take advantage of him/her. At the same time, an assertive person is considerate of other people's feelings and rights. The goal of assertiveness is to get what is wanted without taking advantage of the other person. Assertiveness is acting in your best interest without feeling guilty.

Below are some situations, write down your response to them.

1. You are in a store and you buy your favorite cologne. The clerk gives you change and you leave the store. You find you are two dollars short, what do you do?

2. You are in a nice restaurant and you order a steak rare, and it comes out well done. What is your response?

CHAPTER 9

RELATIONSHIPS

EXERCISE 3

ASSERTIVENESS

Some people are concerned that assertiveness will turn them
into selfish, uncaring, and aggressive manipulators of people.
This idea may be based on some traditional assumptions learned
in childhood. These ideas may keep you locked into a passive
position in relationships.

Listed below is a partial list of mistaken ideas. Make a note
of ones which might fit you.

Mistaken Traditional Beliefs	Your Legtimate rights
1. It is selfish to put your needs before others.	You have a right to put yourself first sometimes.
2. It is shameful to make mistakes. You should have an appropriate response for every occasion.	You have a right to make mistakes.
3. If you can't convince others that your feelings are reasonable, then you must be wrong, or maybe you are going crazy.	You have a right to be the final judge of your feelings and accept them as legitimate.
4. You shouild respect the views of others, especially if they are in a position of authority. Keep your differences of opinion to yourself. Listen and learn.	You have a right to have your own opinions and convictions.
5. You should always try to be logical and consistent.	You have a right to change your mind or decide on a different course of action.
6. You should be flexible and adjust. Others have good reasons for their actions and it's not polite to question them.	You have a right to protest unfair treatment or criticism.
7. You should never interrupt people. Asking questions reveals your stupidity.	You have a right to interrupt in order to ask for clarification.

8. Things could get even worse, don't rock the boat.

You have a right to negotiate for change.

9. You shouldn't take up other's time with your problems.

You have a right to ask for help or emotional support.

10. People don't want to hear that you feel bad, so keep it to yourself.

You have a right to feel and express pain.

11. When someone takes the time to give you advice, you should take it very seriously. They are often right.

You have a right to ignore the advice of others.

12. Knowing that you did something well is its own reward. People don't like showoffs. Successful people are secretly disliked and envied. Be modest when complimented.

You have a right to receive formal recognition for your work and achievements.

13. You should always try to acommmodate others. If you don't, they won't be there when you need them.

You have a right to say "no."

14. Don't be anti-social. People are going to think yoou don't like them if you say you'd rather be alone instead of with them.

You have a right to be alone, even if others would prefer your company.

15. When someone is in trouble, you should help them.

You have a right not to take responsibility for someone else's problem.

16. You should be sensitive to the needs of others, even when they are unable to tell you what they want.

You have a right not to have to anticipate others' needs and wishes.

17. It's always a good policy to stay on people's good side.

You have a right not to always worry about the goodwill of others.

18. It's not nice to put
    people off. If questioned
    give an answer.

You have a right to choose
not to respond to a
situation.

Adapted from:
The Relaxation and Stress Reduction Workbook.

NOTES

RELATIONSHIPS

EXERCISE 4

ASSERTIVENESS

The preceding questionnaire was designed to help raise your level of awareness about your behavior and your ideas which may keep you from getting what you want.

The next step is to target your behavior for change. Of the situations you have looked which do you want to take charge? Pick one which makes you moderately uncomfortable, but with which you have a chance to succeed

Remember, the behavior which is a problem for you is learned. It can be unlearned. Changing behavior is uncomfortable. Most people are fight, confrontation and conflict phobic. Phobias do not get better with avoidance.

Step One: Look at your rights in the situation in question. What is at stake?

Step Two: Define the problem clearly in your own mind. Why is it a problem for you? What needs to be done about it? Is there a clear solution?

Step Three: Set up a time with the person who is involved to discuss the problem.

Step Four: Report clearly the problem you are having. Use I language. Own the problem and discuss without blaming, attacking, pleading, or being too apologetic. Use good eye contact and tell why it is a problem for you.

Step Five: Express a request for a change. What do you want the other person to do about the problem?

Step Six: Reinforce. This means that you must give the other person a reason why it would be to his/her benefit to change. This is the negotiation phase. What will you be willing to do for the other person? Express appreciation for the person's listening and appreciation for the good things in the relationship.

Suggestion:
Discuss only one issue at a time. Do not bring up old wounds or hurts. Do not attack the other person. If the other person

changes the subject, politely call attention to it and bring it back to the problem. Stay in the here and now.

Assertiveness requires practice and awareness. It is easy to slip back into passivity.

EXERCISE 5

MODELS

1. Make a list of all of the qualities in yourself which you feel are most like your father. In which ways are you most like your mother?

2. Make a list of all the negative qualities in yourself. Which parent do these remind you of? What are the ways you are trying to be least like your parents?

3. Make a list of all the ways in which you treat yourself like your parents treated you. Which of these are loving? Which are unloving? What is the one thing you can do to be more loving toward yourself?

4. What are the ways your relationships are a rerun of your parents relationship? What would you most like to change about them?

5. Sit quietly and relax. Let your mind become blank. Visualize your relationshipS in wayS which would be most fulfilling? How do they feel? What are the barriers? Which of these barriers are your responsibility? What do you have the power to change?

EXERCISE 6

INTIMACY

1. These exercises are to be done with a partner. They are designed to create and promote intimate contact, both physically and emotionally. If you become uncomfortable, stop. Learn from the discomfort. Resume when you get comfortable again.

   A. Discuss with your partner the need to have some time together—alone and undisturbed.

   B. Test your comfort zone by asking your partner to stand still. Approach your partner and stop when you find the distance you are most comfortable with. What is the distance between you? This is your bubble. Each person has a zone around them which feels most comfortable. When people get inside that zone they get uncomfortable.

C. Have your partner do the same. Is there a difference in comfort zones? Does it create a problem? Who likes to be closer? More distant?

D. Stand in your comfort zones. Find the optimum level for both of you. Make eye contact. Just look at each other. What do you become aware of? Just look at each other. Look each other up and down. What do you see?

E. Tell your partner what you are aware of as you are looking at him/her. Are you comfortable sharing this awareness? What did you hold back?

F. Tell your partner what you appreciate about him/her. Have your partner do the same. Is it hard to do this? Is it hard for you to receive compliments? Did you believe them?

G. Do you have reservations about your partner? Share one. Have your partner do the same.

H. Do you have concerns about the relationship? What are they? Share one. Have your partner do the same.

NOTES

CHAPTER 9

RELATIONSHIPS

EXERCISE 7

These exercises are designed to help you experience intimacy and pleasure in contact with another. They, like all of the exercises, are created specifically to increase awareness. If you become uncomfortable stop the exercise and explore the discomfort. This will create new awareness and illuminate new areas for growth. When you are involving a partner in these exercises ask your partner's permission and respect his/her right of refusal. Your partner also has the right to discontinue if uncomfortable.

1. Non—demand pleasuring. The goal is to learn to give and receive pleasure.

   A. Ask your partner for a massage. Tell your partner what feels good. This exercise may be done with or without clothing, depending on your comfort level. It does not have to be sexual. It may if you are comfortable with that. The important thing is to receive pleasure. Your partner is to make no demands on you. Just be aware of what feels good, ask for it. Receive it. Take as long as you like.

   B. Change places and now you are the one giving pleasure. What did you learn from this?

People often have difficulty relaxing and pleasuring themselves. Some also have difficulty in letting others do things for them. It is O.K. to ask.

2. **Body Awareness.** Stand before a mirror nude. Look at yourself. What do you see? You are your body. Is your body a source of pleasure? What do you not like about your body? Can you change it? How do you treat your body?

3. What was your family's attitude about nudity? What were your earliest instructions about your body? About sex?

4. Is your body a positive or negative in terms of your self—image? As you look at yourself, take a look at your posture, What do you convey to others through your body language? Confidence, shyness, fear? Try

experimenting with your posture, see if you can adopt a stance of power and confidence. How does that feel?

5. Pay attention to the areas of tension, discomfort, and pain in your body. Where do you store your feelings when stressed?

NOTES

CHAPTER 9

RELATIONSHIPS

EXERCISE 8

When do you behave non—assertively?

Asking for help.

Stating a difference of opinion.

Receiving and expressing negative feelings.

Receiving and expressing positive feelings.

Dealing with someone who refuses to cooperate.

Speaking up about something that annoys you.

Talking when all eyes are on you.

Protesting a rip—off.

Saying "no".

Responding to undeserved criticism.

Making requests of authority figures.

Negotiating for something you want.

Having to take charge.

Asking for cooperation.

Proposing an idea.

Taking charge.

Asking questions.

Dealing with attempts at manipulation.

Asking for service.

Asking for a date or appointment.

Asking for favors.

Other_____

Who are the people with whom you are non—assertive?

Parents

Fellow workers, classmates

Strangers

Old friends

Spouse or mate

Employer

Relatives

Children

Acquaintances

Clerks, hired help

More than two or three people in a group

Other_____

What do you want that you have been unable to achieve with non—assertive styles?

Approval for things you have done well.

To get help with certain tasks.

More attention or time with your mate.

To be listened to and understood.

To make boring or frustrating situations more satisfying.

To not have to be nice all the time.

Confidence in speaking up when something is important to you.

Greater comfort with strangers, store clerks, mechanics,etc..

Confidence in asking for contact with people you find attractive.

Getting a new job, asking for interviews, raises, etc..

Comfort with people who supervise you, or work under you.

To not feel angry and bitter a lot of the time.

Overcome a feeling of helplessness and the sense that nothing ever really changes.

Initiating satisfying sexual experiences.

Do something totally different and novel

Getting time by yourself.

Doing things that are fun or relaxing for you.

Other_____

NOTES

CHAPTER 9

RELATIONSHIPS

FURTHER READING

Alberti, Robert E. and Emmons, Michael. Your Perfect Right. San Luis Obispo: Impact Press. 1974.

Bach, George R, and Wyden, Peter. The Intimate Enemy. New York: William Morrow. 1969.

Bower, Sharon, and Bower, Gordon. Asserting Yourself. Reading, Mass: Addison—Wesley. 1970.

Davis, Martha. Eshelman, Elizabeth, and McKay, Mathew. The Relaxation and Stress Reduction Workbook, Third Edition. Oakland, CA: New Harbinger Pub., 1988.

Fensterheim, Herbert and Baer. Don't Say Yes When You Want To Say No. New York: David McKay. 1975.

Fromm, Erik. The Art of Loving. New York: Bantam Books. 1963.

Lieberman, Mendel, and Harie, Marion. Resolving Family and Other Conflicts. Santa Cruz, Ca: Unity Press. 1981.

Smith, Manuel J. When I Say No, I Feel Guilty. New York: The Dial Press. 1975.

Yalom, Irvin D. Existential Psychotherapy. New York: Basic Books. 1980.

CHAPTER 10

WORKING THE PROGRAM

Many alcoholics who have relapsed did so because they were so dysfunctional in their recovery that the pain became so severe as to lead to one of three choices, (1) return to using, (2) suicide, (3) insanity. For them, relalpse seemed the best option.   Terence Gorski

Addiction is a disorder characterized by **RELAPSE**.   Thus begin many books and articles on the subject of addiction. Others define the success of recovery as the lack of relapse. I believe there are a number of important underlying assumptions involved in these statements which need to be discussed; assumptions that are the basis of the very nature of recovery.   Is relapse inevitable?   If a person relapses, does it mean he or she is a failure and isn't recovered?   If a person is sober, are they recovered?   We have often heard the phrases in reference to relapse—"he slipped", "he fell off the wagon".   Again, these phrases imply a certain view of addiction and recovery.   In this case, the implication is that relapse is something inevitable that happens to everyone.   In fact, the statistics support the conclusion that a great number of people do relapse.   The data are 54% still had problems 4 years after starting recovery and that only 28% were free of substance abuse 4 years after beginning a recovery program.   The majority of individuals who have substance abuse problems "were highly unstable in their ability to refrain from problem usage." Many are likely to relapse several times and be involved in numerous programs.

These statistics are disheartening and the problem of relapse is one that causes health care providers and third party payers to refuse to provide coverage for the problem. In fact, it is a big problem. In fact, it is costly. In fact, relapse is likely and anyone who is involved in the field of addiction is aware that it can be a discouraging, frustrating experience to work with addicts. A more glaring fact is that it is even more discouraging and costly to the ones who are struggling to achieve sobriety and fail in spite of their best efforts to find a way to recover from this diabolical disorder. Because there is failure, frustration, and even multiple relapses only testifies to the deverity of the problem with which we are dealing, it does not mean it impossible and that we should throw up our hands it just means that we must redouble our efforts at finding more effective ways of dealing with the problem. Our failures are testament that we do not understand the problem. Many find it easier to explain failed recovery by blaming the victim.

I believe that relapse prevention begins by thoroughly understanding the problem and then dispelling many of the mistaken beliefs, myths and misunderstandings about this very complicated process. Many of our ideas about relapse prevention have originated from the work of Terence Gorski, who interviewed hundreds of relapsed alcoholics. He found there were many common characteristics which were recognizable patterns. Because of his work we now know more about the problem. Gorski is convinced that myths and mistaken beliefs result in faulty and dysfunctional recovery. He categorized these erroneous ideas into 4 areas:

(1) Mistaken beliefs about relapse.

(2) Mistaken ideas about sobriety.

(3) Mistaken ideas about treatment.

(4) Mistaken ideas about motivation.

(5) I would add, mistaken beliefs about addiction.

These mistaken beliefs affect how the addict relates to the problem and subsequently goes about living. For example, if an addict has the mistaken idea that sobriety is recovery: that abstinence is all it takes, then the focus is on use or non—use. If you don't use, you are recovered, if you use, then you have relapsed.

I concur with Gorski, that sobriety is the precondition for recovery. The danger in equating abstinence with recovery is that it obscures the fact that once one has gotten sober, there are a whole host of problems waiting to be solved. It's as if the addict believes—"I am fine as long as I don't use, because this proves I am in control." This attitude leads to dysfunctional recovery and probable relapse.

It is clear, then, that our ideas about relapse and recovery are co—determining. So let us proceed by looking at my original definition of Recovery. In my model, recovery is a journey, a process in which we are committed to taking responsibility for our lives. And that the goal of recovery is too live authentically in relationship to ourselves and others; without having to resort to the use of chemicals to cope. In order to do this, we must surround ourselves with a caring community and live with the power that comes from the awareness of the sacredness of life, *Recovery is a way of life!*

With this model in mind, let us look at the problem of relapse. First of all, the disorder of addiction is viewed as a problem with multiple causes. So when a person relapses there are probably several reasons for this occurrence.

Is relapse inevitable? Again, there are many mistaken beliefs about this. Our view of it will determine our recovery strategies. For example, if one believes that relapse just spontaneously and magically occurs without warning, one is likely to believe there is nothing that can be done. Clearly, this faulty assumption leads to feelings of helplessness and hopelessness. It also tends to lead to the belief that it just happens and that it had nothing to do with you.

The facts are that relapse is preventable and that there are many well understood warning signs; therefore there is a great deal that can be done to prevent relapse. For example, a typical relapse pattern is: (1) to begin thinking about using again, (2) a compulsion to use develops, (3) high risk situations and behaviors are engaged in, and finally (4) recovery activities are discontinued. The danger is that these warning signs occur late in the process and are often met with denial. "I know what I am doing, I know when I am in danger. See, I am in control."

Relapse must be met with realistic expectations. Many do not expect to ever have a problem again. What my goal of treatment for any disorder consists of is teaching my clients to manage their lives more effectively. That includes being able to work with their symptoms of depression, anxiety, or relationship crises in such a way that they do not become disabling. The goal is competency and self—management; not perfection. By establishing more realistic espectations there is less likelihood of being highly self-critical if the expectations are not met. This leads to more realistic problem solving and less shame and guilt.

What this means in practical terms is that getting sober is merely the first step in recovery. It is also a precondition for recovery. I have not seen anyone successfully recover who continued to use mind and mood altering substances. This means that sobriety is not enough: that those who are the most successful in recovery are the ones who make the commitment to healing their wounds, learning necessary living skills and solving whatever problems contributed to the addiction in the first place.

This is the fundamental conviction of **STEPCARE**. That recovery means establishing a solid psychological foundation which will make it possible to live without chemicals.

Just as recovery is a process which can be understood and learned, so too is relapse. Relapse prevention is a process that can lead to the implementation of effective and intelligent strategies for recovery and for living. When they are incorporated into every day life they are more effective.

In order to fully address relapse, we need to consider a number of inter—related factors:

    (1) Individual personality factors.

    (2) Unique environmental stressors.

    (3) Attitudes about drugs and alcohol.

    (4) Social pressures.

    (5) Available support.

    (6) Age and history of addiction.

    (7) Family factors.

This broad range of behavior has been called "The Relapse Syndrome" by Gorski. Without going into a lengthy discussion of his excellent description, I would like to summarize it as briefly as possible. Once again, we can view the Relapse Syndrome as affecting behavior, thoughts, and feelings.

Gorski's view of recovery is that it is like walking up the down escalator, One can never stand still. In actuality, if one is not actively working at recovery, one is unknowingly creating the conditions for relapse.

Why is this true? I believe it is because abstinence leads to being faced with all the problems which were masked by addiction, Abstinence means giving up the primary coping tool, This leads to distress, dysfunction and misery; "Dysfunctional Sobriety". Gorski reports that many alcoholics who have relapsed did so because they were so dysfunctional in recovery that it seemed to lead to only 1 of 3 choices: (1) suicide, (2) insanity, or (3) return to using. For them, using seemed to be the best choice.

The problem for many is the management of the "Post Acute Withdrawal Phase of addiction." In this phase, the addict is struggling with all of the diverse and interrelated complications and consequences of addiction, These, of course, have to do with the neurological, organic, social, psychological, economic, and relational side effects. Cravings and the Post Acute Withdrawal can take several years to completely subside. Given the number and complexity of these problems it is little wonder that relapse occurs.

Gorski describes **PAWS** as symptoms which result in (1) difficulty in clear thinking, problems with memory, judgement and abstract reasoning (problem solving), (2) feeling management; numb, overactive or inappropriate responses, (3) stress related problems and (4) poor psycho—motor coordination. Many of these symptoms are because of the neurological effects of chemicals, and others are because of the psychological stresses and crises created by addiction. Remember our discussion on stress: it effects the whole person.

It should come as no surprise, then, that relapse is highly probable in the initial stages of recovery because the physiology of addiction is strong, motivation is tenuous, attachment to a program is weak, and stress from the consequence of use is high. Furthermore, guilt, shame and remorse are battering self—esteem and social support may have been alienated, and is therefore, non—existent. The stress of discontinued chemical use, the effort to achieve sobriety and the wreckage or havoc created by the addiction may prove

279

overwhelming. This is a very vulnerable period when maximum support and structure are necessary. Survival truly is moment to moment and then a day at a time. It's like the old joke, when you are up to your ass in alligators it is difficult to remember the larger objective was to do an ecological survey of the swamp. So too, early sobriety is characterized by crises and instability and creation of a long term recovery program seems impossibly far away. But eventually the emphasis will begin to shift from mere sobriety to recovery.

To summarize, relapse may be very likely in the post acute phase of sobriety because the recovering person is weakest physically, and psychologically, while at the same time being faced with what may feel like overwhelming stressors. All of this while being deprived of a chemical crutch. Failure, then, to manage the aftermath of addiction is a prime reason for relapse. The interactive effects of PAWS and increased stress can make a person feel crazy, dysfunctional, helpless, confused, and anxious. This is one reason it is crucial to have maximum support at this phase of the crisis.

In many ways, recovery from addiction parallels the recovery process of trauma victims. There is the acute crisis of the trauma, then the immediate aftermath of the crisis and the final stage of normalizing the life. Gorski describes the process in a similar vein. The first phase is getting sober, stage 2 is managing the crisis of withdrawal, stage 3 is managing PAWS, stage 4 is dealing with the bio—psycho—social effects of addiction (aftermath) and finally, stage 5 is a recovery lifestyle; (normalizing).

Normalizing life is where the work of rebuilding begins: restoring self—esteem, rebuilding shattered relationships and dealing with problems related to work and financial instability. Learning to handle depression, anxiety, stress, anger, shame, guilt, remorse and hopelessness is difficult to do when it feels like you are just barely keeping yourself together. This is when recovery begins with the need to learn new, more effective coping skills, build an effective, support network of sponsors, meetings, recovery support groups, and if necessary, psychotherapy.

This part of the recovery process is much like the grief work that I have my clients do who have suffered a loss of a loved one. In many ways, giving up an addiction is a very significant loss. There is a great deal of loss, sadness, anger and denial centering around the lost love on which we were so dependent. It is no longer available to us for comfort; we feel angry, frightened, tense and empty without it. For many addicts the addiction was the only thing they had left. Life is organized around the lover and friend on whom the addict has become totally dependent. And, also like a death, life seems purposeless, we are lost and don't know what to do without the daily activities of using. We lose the rituals, ceremonies, activities, and friendships associated with using when we give it up. Life becomes disorganized.

The initial phases of recovery are also like grieving. First there is denial, then bargaining, as we try to find a way to manage the addiction without losing it. We try various strategies of clinging and holding onto this destructive lover. Then there is rage at not being like others. We ask ourselves, "Why?" and "Why me?" We feel immensely sorry for ourselves. This is the period of feeling victimized by the fates. This slides easily into depression and despair as we continue to come to grips with the loss and reality the problem has created.

Grieving is a necessary process if we are to get to the next stage which is fundamental to recovery: *Acceptance.* This is not a once and for all step. Just as in grief, we go from step 1 to step 4 all in one day and may get terribly stuck in rage for a long period of time. But with work, support and care, we can get through it.

The subsequent stages cannot be accomplished without grief work, acceptance and relinquishing the beloved. We cannot get on with rebuilding our lives without giving up the addictive substance.

Remember, successful recovery is dependent on the quality of the recovery environment. In my model of recovery I see relapse and recovery at opposite ends of a polarity. (see chart)

If a person is moving toward recovery, there will be indications of success in several areas. These markers tell us we are headed in the right direction: **(1) self—esteem, (2) relationships, (3) stress indicators, (4) cognitive signs, and (5) the feeling or affective domain.** In the Recovery Relapse Chart I believe it is rather easy to quickly get a sense of the troublesome areas and be able to chart the progress one is making. Obviously, if one sees a decrease in relationships, self—esteem, and increases in depression, stress and denial, it should quickly trigger warning lights that if the trend continues the person is headed for a relapse. The key is monitoring recovery progress. Dysfunction, if not dealt with, can trigger relapse.

By tracking one's progress, it is possible to increase awareness of work well done, and areas that need to be targeted for improvement. This is how an overall recovery strategy is developed. Let us examine some specific strategies which can be employed to prevent relapse or if it does occur, prevent it from being a prolonged and destructive episode.

I believe the single most important tool a recovering person needs in their arsenal is *AWARENESS.* This should be a familiar concept by now. *AWARENESS* is the antidote to denial. If we are practicing denial, we are living blindly. In addition to being blinded and deluded by denial, lack of awareness also cuts us off from our feelings. Living in awareness means being open to our inner life as well as that which is going on around us.

This step is *ASSESSMENT.* Feeling the feelings, tracking them down and then interrogating them leads to understanding their meaning. Remember, feelings are messages. When we assess them, we are able to more appropriately deal with them without resorting to the use of mind and mood altering substances. What do we do when we feel shame and hate ourselves? That's the important question. The target is shame and our damaged self—esteem. We need to reframe these old feelings into an action strategy of positive self—talk,

ASSESSMENT OF RELAPSE POTENTIAL

Rate the following factors on a 5 point rating scale. From very Unsatisfactory to very Satisfactory.

1. SELF—ESTEEM

1 ____   2 ____   3 ____   4 ____   5 ____

VERY UNSATISFACTORY, UNSATISFACTORY, STABLE, SATISFACTORY, VERY SATISFACTORY

2. VOCATION

1 ____   2 ____   3 ____   4 ____   5 ____

3. RELATIONSHIPS

1 ____   2 ____   3 ____   4 ____   5 ____

4. FAMILY (Wife, Children)

1 ____   2 ____   3 ____   4 ____   5 ____

5. FAMILY (Mother, Father, Siblings)

1 ____   2 ____   3 ____   4 ____   5 ____

6. FINANCIAL CONDITIONS

1 ____   2 ____   3 ____   4 ____   5 ____

7. DEPRESSION

1 ____   2 ____   3 ____   4 ____   5 ____

8. ANXIETY

1 ____   2 ____   3 ____   4 ____   5 ____

9. CRAVINGS

1 ____   2 ____   3 ____   4 ____   5 ____

10. PHYSICAL HEALTH

1 ____   2 ____   3 ____   4 ____   5 ____

11. SPIRITUALITY

1 ____   2 ____   3 ____   4 ____   5 ____

12. STRESS

    1 ____   2 ____   3 ____   4 ____   5 ____

13. RECOVERY PROGRAM

    1 ____   2 ____   3 ____   4 ____   5 ____

14. PLEASURE (Hobbies, Recreation)

    1 ____   2 ____   3 ____   4 ____   5 ____

15. SLEEP

    1 ____   2 ____   3 ____   4 ____   5 ____

16. APPETITE

    1 ____   2 ____   3 ____   4 ____   5 ____

17. EXERCISE

    1 ____   2 ____   3 ____   4 ____   5 ____

18. ANGER

    1 ____   2 ____   3 ____   4 ____   5 ____

19. SHAME - GUILT

    1 ____   2 ____   3 ____   4 ____   5 ____

20. HOPE

    1 ____   2 ____   3 ____   4 ____   5 ____

NOTES

active forgiveness of ourselves and positive affirmations about our recovery successes. This will lead to further healing of old wounds as well as heading off an immediate crisis. Beating ourselves up leads to use, not healing.

This kind of awareness leads to self—knowledge. Know thyself—is an ancient injunction but very valid for our purposes. We need to know our vulnerabilities. If you have diligently worked your way through this book, then you have acquired a great deal of knowledge about yourself and how you have come to be the way you are. With this kind of awareness, you are now better prepared to deal with high risk situations and have a better understanding of your triggers. If you know what your weak spots and triggers are, it is possible to design coping strategies for avoiding trouble.

Awareness can be enhanced by learning the skill of *Tracking.* Tracking merely means using your awareness and focused attention to pay particular attention to yourself when you are having trouble with something. For example, you were troubled by a feeling of depression and apprehension after you told a friend about your addiction. It feels like you are sliding into a lonely place where you start having thoughts of self—criticism, shame, and hopelessness; tracking these feelings is essential to regaining your self—esteem.

Tracking means being able to identify when the feelings began and what they might be about. Let's say that the feelings triggered embarrassment and vulnerability for sharing something you are not proud of. These feelings easily stir up old feelings of shame and hurt related to early parental shaming. By being able to track the origin of these feelings and identify their meaning, it is possible to move to the next step in intervention.

Notice how awareness leads naturally to problem solving and then action strategies designed to deal with the problem. Take a moment to reflect on how you might have handled these feelings of shame, guilt and embarrassment before.

Again, the key is living with awareness which leads to action based on our accurate assessment of the situation, Know yourself, your triggers, and your high risk situations.

A very important tool in your recovery program is your support system. I cannot emphasize enough the importance of a quality recovery environment which is populated by caring, non—judgmental, supportive people who genuinely understand the problems you are having. It may take a long time to develop this part of your recovery program. It takes a while to build confidence and trust. It is even more difficult for addicts because we typically do not handle relationships very well. But this is good, because it forces us into the very thing we fear most—*INTIMACY.*

By working this area of the program we are working on several problems at the same time. In order to build a relationship we have to reach out and—oh—pain—let someone know we hurt and-oh-pain-need help. This requires motivation, learning to trust, and it also overcomes self—hatred and low self—esteem. It is very difficult to accept care and love when we don't feel lovable and in fact are filled with self—loathing and disgust. It is easier to do it with those you know have been in the same place — the fellowship of revovering people (A.A.) (N.A.) or some other recovery program.

In brief, relapse is something which may occur in the life of any recovering person. Being forewarned is to be forearmed, It is better to acknowledge the possibility than to be in denial by asserting that "I will never slip, or fall off the wagon." This kind of thinking only leads to relapse and then the shame, guilt, remorse, damaged health and self—esteem. This is the natural consequence of thinking we are immortal only to discover once again we are all to human.

In summary, look for warning signs: changes in behavior, changes in attitudes, changes in feelings and moods and in particular changes in thoughts. None of these are significant in themselves, but may be meaningful if you notice familiar patterns which have led to relapse before.

Being upset, thinking about using, hanging out with old friends after you have ended a relationship are not a sign of relapse, but they could very well alert you to the fact you need to heed the warning before it goes to the next step. Know thyself, be true to yourself and work the program!

As I think about the relapse process, I think of those clients I have worked with who have relapsed, and I think of those times in my own life when I have failed to live up to my own expectations as well as disappointed others. The most often asked question is "What to do when the program isn't working. What do I do when I have relapsed?" Rather than feel hopeless and helpless: work the program!

Once again, I believe the best strategy is not to ask the question after it has happened. If you ask yourself what will I do if, or when, I relapse, you have a much better chance of dealing with it if it occurs. Why? Because it is very difficult to come up with a meaningful strategy during a crisis. Recently I consulted with a major airport on disaster response strategies. I found that the key is preparedness and planning. It is too late to buy the crash trucks and work out the emergency response agreements between police, fire and medical organizations after a disaster. I believe the same is also true in psychological crises. Obviously, we do not want to create one crises after another so we can get good at it. Although that would seem to be what many of us do inadvertently.

With all of this serving as a prelude. let us look briefly at some ways that these concepts can be translated into a specific action plan for relapse prevention.

Again, it needs to be emphasized that any relapse prevention program is not some separate and special thing a person does when the cravings get strong. Relapse is unnecessary, it comes from dysfunctional living which is mistaken for sobriety. It stems from lack of awareness, ignorance about recovery, lack of knowledge about relapse warning signs, not having a workable recovery plan, and not dealing with powerful underlying feelings which may sabotage recovery. I believe that the development of a workable recovery program will have incorporated within it planning for relapse and ways to minimize its destructive potential.

Using my simple formula of **Awareness, Assessment,** and **Action** let's see how we might translate this into specifics.

STEP (1) **AWARENESS**

The goal here is to use awareness as an antidote for denial and lack of information. Relapse education, warning sign identification, doing daily inventories, and keeping a recovery journal all serve to keep the focus on living with a high level of awareness.

I would also suggest that attending meetings and being a part of a recovery group also will serve the purpose of continuing your personal growth and learning more effective coping skills.

Again, if you have as your basic commitment the development of a whole person and healing relationships you will be moving in the right direction. Awareness and mind altering substances are mutually exclusive.

Step (2) **ASSESSMENT**

Assessment builds on those skills we have been working on in this program. The goal is to use awareness in a way that generates meaningful information about yourself.

As I have said before, by learning to track the symptoms, make sense of the feelings, analyze our behavior, thoughts and decisions, we will be less likely to be impulsive, compulsive, and self—destructive.

Inventory training is a good solid tool for developing our powers of observation. This will enable us to make good plans, set realistic goals and stop the merciless self—criticism of shame and guilt.

Decoding and recognizing warning signs also serves to derail relapse before it picks up momentum. Relapse thrives on lack of awareness and stinking thinking. It's like a mushroom, it thrives under similar circumstances. Assessment requires development of self—monitoring skills. This is the essence of effective living.

Step (3) **ACTION**

Action means just what it says. It is active rather than passive. It means owning our behavior and taking responsibility for decisions and their consequences. Action is the antidote for victimization. Action is empowerment! But it must be intelligent action.

Action is imperative for crisis resolution and stabilizing your life. It is the only way you can regain control. Action is essential for managing the symptoms of PAWS and going beyond sobriety.

Some action steps include simple things like (1) verbalizing feelings to a friend or sponsor, (2) venting pent up feelings, (3) actively checking reality by seeking feedback from trusted people, (4) set goals, make plans and problem solve, (5) track—learn from mistakes, (6) educate—learn as much as you can about your problem, become an expert on recovery—this will increase competence and control, (7) manage stress — learn effective coping skills, and (8) stabilize your life through active caretaking of your body (diet, exercise, nicotine, caffeine, sugar) and your relationships.

This last item bears emphasizing because it is the foundation of recovery: *active self—care*. This is the most empowering thing you can do. A very important part of self—care is including family members in recovery. Taking this step will create reconciliation, healing and make the family a powerful ally in recovery.

Since addiction involves entire families, it is essential that all those affected be involved in making the changes which lead to recovery. It is a very simple truism, when one person changes, the whole family system is thrown out of balance. This is true whether the changes are positive or negative. Co—dependency or co—addiction require everyone in the family working on the appropriate life style changes which become the goal of recovery. The family should also be included in all recovery plans and relapse prevention planning.

If relapse occurs in spite of your efforts to the contrary, the next step is to think of what to do about it. The goal is to stop it as quickly as possible. The longer it goes on the greater the likelihood it will not be a relapse episode, but a return to continual use of drugs or alcohol. This is a very important choice point. It is very difficult to come up with the necessary motivation to stop once you have started again.

This is why a contingency plan is essential. Discuss it with your therapist, sponsor, friend or significant other. Tell them what you want them to do if they suspect relapse or even if they see you heading for a fall. So much of this depends on you. If you are really bent on using and doing a big thing, you're not likely to tell anyone because you really don't want to be stopped or have anyone interfere with your run.

It is a matter of attitude. How destructive are you? Are you convinced that you are an addict? Are you convinced it is destructive to use and that when you use you cannot control it? The next question is, how are you going to treat yourself after a relapse? Most respond with guilt, shame, remorse and embarrassment. These are very appropriate emotions. We probably should feel stupid after doing things we know will hurt us and the people we care about. So the strategy is learning to deal with ourselves when we are angry and disappointed with ourselves. The key in relapse is to get stopped as quickly as possible. The combination of guilt, shame, and continued use can and will be a vicious cycle of self—hatred which leads to self—abuse and eventual suicide or death by overdose whether it is intentional or not.

Realistic appraisal is the key. It is important to admit the relapse, stop it as quickly as possible and begin the recovery process all over again, The next step is a post mortem. Learn from the relapse. Beating yourself up only makes you feel worse and it interferes with recovery. You cannot recover by beating up on yourself. Self—hatred keeps you from asking the important questions, like "what happened?" "What did I do wrong?" "What could I have done differently?" "Why now?" "What problem was I trying to solve?" "What am I trying to avoid?" What emotion was I expressing in this manner?

If you have difficulty getting stopped on your own, then

you must seek the level of care necessary to get stopped. A professional assessment is probably essential to determine the necessity of detox. Stopping suddenly after prolonged heavy usage is putting yourself in medical danger. It is essential to stop and do damage control. Try to minimize the consequences of the relapse by doing whatever it takes to stop and get back on track again. It is up to you to seek the level of care necessary to get the job done. By having a list of recovery resources in your plan, you are a step ahead of the game. Recovery programs, recovery homes, detox and treatment facilities, therapists and physicians are all easier to locate ahead of time than when you are in the midst of a full—blown crisis. This kind of realistic planning is also another mark of maturing in your recovery.

Once the crisis is handled, it is important to take a look at your overall recovery program. Take a look at what works and what is not working. It is very simple; do what works, and stop doing what doesn't work. Recovery programs need to be flexible and adaptable. You will need to change your program depending on where you are in the recovery process. The program is working best when it is meeting your needs. Only you can know what you need at a given time. This is where we are responsible for our own recovery. The good news is, it is up to me and the bad news is no one can do it but me. Working the program is for life, and recovery is living fully. As we live our lives one step at a time, we learn the meaning of caring. This is the nature of the Hero's Journey.

CHAPTER 10

WORKING THE PROGRAM

EXERCISE 1

CREATING A STRATEGY FOR RECOVERY

We have reviewed triggers, risk factors and vulnerabilities and suggested coping strategies. In order for any program to have meaning, it must be very personal—it must work for you. Recovery is a long—term process. It works best when it becomes a part of you and becomes a way of life.

Make a list of changes you want to make.

1.   6.

2.   7.

3.   8.

4.   9.

5.   10.

Make a list of short term goals for yourself.

1.   6.

2.   7.

3.   8.

4.   9.

5.   10.

CHAPTER 10

WORKING THE PROGRAM

EXERCISE 2

RECOVERY PLAN

Make a list of long term goals you want to accomplish:

Make a list of signs that you are making progress.
In other words, how will you know you are accomplishing your
goals?

I will know I am recovering because:

1.

2.

3.

4.

5.

My friends and family will know I am making progress
because:

1.

2.

3.

4.

5.

WORKING THE PROGRAM

EXERCISE 3

RECOVERY PLAN

LIFESTYLE MANAGEMENT

Define for yourself those areas of your life which are satisfactory and which you feel are your assets for recovery.

Example: work, friends, family, hobbies, religious activities, school, career, civic activities.

Review the areas of your life where you feel there is instability, or lack of balance.

How will you bring these into balance?

What steps are you willing to take to maintain your sobriety?

1.   7.

2.   8.

3.   9.

4.   10.

5.   11.

6.   12.

CHAPTER 10

WORKING THE PROGRAM

EXERCISE 4

Make a list of recovery resources which you are willing to
make a commitment to using.

Therapist Appointment

Time   Date

A.A. or N.A. Meetings

Number of times per week

Location   Day/Time of Meetings

Alanon—Alateen Meetings for family members

Finding a Sponsor by   Date

Phone Number

Make a list of emergency people and their phone numbers you
can call when you are in need of support or are in danger of
relapse. Keep it with you.

WORKING THE PROGRAM

EXERCISE 5

TRACKING

Since you began your recovery have you had a period of relapse? If so, answer the following questions:

1. What happened? Describe without judging.

2. What led up to the episode? What specific clues can you identify which preceded your relapse?

3. How much time elapsed between the buildup of signals to your actual return to using?

4. What did you learn? Can you identify alternative strategies for preventing relapse?

CHAPTER 10

WORKING THE PROGRAM

EXERCISE 6

TRACKING

Identify Your High Risk Situations
Check the ones that apply

1. **Social Situations**

   A. Being invited to parties where alcohol or drugs are likely to be present.

   B. Being invited to stop by a bar after work to socialize.

   C. Most of my old friends use alcohol or drugs.

   D. Being around others who are having a good time using alcohol or drugs.

   E. All the executives at work party and you want to succeed at work and are included in the get togethers.

   F. Other Pressures.

2. **Relationships**

   A. I have blown all my friendships.

   B. I am shy and a loner.

   C. I have difficulty developing relationships.

   D. People don't seem to like me.

   E. Difficulty in trusting and being close.

   F. Conflicts and anger are hard to handle.

   G. My significant other—partner—spouse—doesn't trust me and is nagging and playing policeman.

   H. Being comfortable sober at parties is difficult.

   I. Sexual activity without alcohol or drugs is difficult.

J. The responsibilities of marriage are too much for me.

K. I don't know how to relate to, discipline, or play with my children.

L. Others

3. Recovery Programs

A. I can't seem to find any program where I feel comfortable

B. I don't need help.

C. I find it hard to be consistent in attending A.A. or N.A.

D. Working the program is a pain. It is difficult and I would rather do other things.

E. My family doesn't want to be involved in "my problem."

F. I don't like to talk about my problems with others.

G. Treatment is not helping me.

H. Nothing works, I have tried everything.

I. Other program difficulties.

4. High Risk Situations

A. Work stress triggers cravings.

B. Unstructured time — weekends, holidays, create anxiety and tension.

C. I don't know how to have fun with out it.

D. I miss being able to celebrate or party.

E. Being alone fills me with dread and anxiety.

F. I feel overwhelmed by all the problems I have created.

G. I can't seem to sleep or relax without it.

H. Family reunions and contact with parents.

5. **Internal Risks**

   A. Anxiety — panic episodes.

   B. Depression — need something to get me up.

   C. Mood swings — I feel so unstable.

   D. Stress and pressure.

   E. Shame, guilt — I hate my life.

   F. Low self—esteem. Feeling doomed helpless and like perpetual loser.

   G. Anger and resentment.

   H. Poor impulse control:

   Obsessive thoughts
   Compulsive behavior
   Gambling, eating, spending, working

   I. Loneliness—emptiness.

   J. Lack of meaning, direction, purpose.

   K. Apathy.

   L. Always disappointed with self and others.

   M. Memories, flashbacks and old wounds.

6. **Physical**

   A. Physical exhaustion.

   B. Disturbed sleep patterns.

   C. No Exercise.

   D. Excessive caffeine intake.

   E. Tobacco Addiction.

   F. Not eating.

   G. Eating excessively.

   H. Irritability.

I. Agitation, excessive energy, feeling wired.

J. Physical Pain.

K. Constant worrying — unable to shut off troubling thoughts.

L. Explosive rages.

M. Other

NOTES

CHAPTER 10

WORKING THE PROGRAM

EXERCISE 8

TARGETING

Review all of the high risk factors you have identified. Make a list of the ones you feel are the most difficult for you. Ones, which, in your judgement are likely to contribute to a relapse.

List your top 10

1.   6.

2.   7.

3.   8.

4.   9.

5.   10.

Take each one of these and write down as much as you know about it: the who, what, where and how of it.

CHAPTER 10

WORKING THE PROGRAM

EXERCISE 9

TARGETING

CRAVINGS — URGES TO USE

Review a time when you felt a particularly strong urge or craving. Describe it:

What were you doing at the time?

What was going on around you?

What were the physical signs?

What were the psychological signs?

Make a list of quick remedies for cravings. Something you can do immediately to stop it. For example (1) exercise, (2) talk to a friend, (3) go to a meeting, (4) distractions.

CHAPTER 10

WORKING THE PROGRAM

EXERCISE 10

TARGETING

Now that you have identified 10 of your personal risks, take a moment to see which ones you are presently having difficulty with. Define it:

High Risk One:

High Risk Two:

For each high risk situation, think of a way — a coping strategy for dealing with it. Review the chapter in this book to refresh your memory if necessary.

Coping strategy — what you can do.

1.

2.

3.

4.

5.

CHAPTER 10

WORKING THE PROGRAM

EXERCISE 11

TARGETING

Now that you have reviewed the various areas in this book, is there one area or more where you feel you need more work?

Describe that area:

Based on your growing self—awareness, what do you need to do about this area of vulnerability. View it as an area for growth and challenge.

Strategy for Growth:

CHAPTER 10

WORKING THE PROGRAM

RELAPSE PREVENTION STRATEGIES

SUMMARY

Use this sheet as a checklist to review what you need to do in your planning. Remember, planning is prevention.

STEP 1   AWARENESS

1. Relapse education.

2. Warning sign identification.

3. Identifying, expressing feelings.

4. Journaling.

5. Daily inventory.

STEP 2   ASSESSMENT

1. Tracking high risk situations.

2. Inventory training – Goal review.

3. Recovery program – update.

4. Recording and decoding warning signs.

STEP 3   ACTION

1. Crisis Management
   Call Sponsor   Call Therapist
   Talk to Friend   Go to a meeting
   Go to detox

2. Seek Support
   Find and attend a twelve step meeting regularly
   Join recovery support group
   Go to a therapist
   Involve family in therapy
   Get a sponsor

3. Lifestyle Changes
   Work on self—esteem   Eat Healthy Diet
   Learn self—monitoring skills   Work regular hours
   Find a spiritual community   Excercise
   Learn stress management skills
   Develop support network of sober friends

308

CHAPTER 10

WORKING THE PROGRAM

FURTHER READING

Daley, Dennis C. Relapse Prevention Workbook. Holmes Beach Fla: Learning Publications, 1986.

Gorski, Terence and Miller, Merlene. Learning to Live Again: Guidelines for Recovery. Kansas: Human Ecology Systems, 1982.

Gorski, Terence and Miller, Merlene. Staying Sober: A Guide for Relapse Prevention. Missouri: Independence Press, 1986.

Wegscheider, Sharon. Another Change: Hope for the Alcoholic Family. California: Science and Behavior Books, 1981.

Woititz, Jane. Adult Children of Alcoholics. Florida: Health Communications Inc., 1983.

NOTES

CHAPTER 11

THE HEROE'S JOURNEY

IN CHOOSING YOUR GOD, YOU CHOOSE
YOUR WAY OF LOOKING AT THE UNIVERSE
THERE ARE PLENTY OF GODS
CHOOSE YOURS
THE GOD YOU WORSHIP
IS THE GOD YOU DESERVE
JOSEPH CAMPBELL

In the 1600's Galileo and the church came into conflict over the nature of truth and physical reality. Galileo was demonstrating, through the scientific method, that the earth and man were not the center of "God's" universe. This contradicted theological dogma of that time. The problem then, was all truth came from the church as revealed truth. The problem now, ironically, four hundred years later is as if the roles are reversed. Galileo is now coming to the spiritual leaders and saying, "there is only one truth and that truth comes from science. Science is the new god and Spirit does not exist because it cannot be empirically demonstrated.

The problem of Galileo and the church illustrates for me the difficulty we face as dwellers in the expanded cosmos, merely hinted at by Galileo. What does it do to our image of ourselves to be a bit of star dust in an infinitely vast and incomprehensibly old universe? Is it still possible to have a sense of awe and mystery when science reduces everything to cause and effect? What has been lost and what has been gained by raising science to the level of dogma? Has science and the scientist become the secular priesthood? Has science so secularized our world that Faith is no longer relevanat or possible?

As I look at the problems we have today, I see the effect of the scientific and technological revolution begun by Galileo having an effect in three ways. The first is on our belief systems; our faith. Secondly, our sense of community and thirdly, our individual identity.

Modern theologians and philosophers have concerned themselves with these questions and have likened it to stripping the earth of mystery. Some—Nietzsche for one, have called it the death of God. Others, Sartre and Camus, have characterized our existence as absurd; without meaning.

Joseph Campbell, our most notable chronicler of myths and mythology, has reasoned that many of our contemporary problems are a result of the ancient beliefs, rituals, myths and symbols losing their power. At both the cultural and the personal level, then, the loss of faith and meaning presents an unusual dilemma and challenge for us today.

By that I mean because of the impact of science and technology we find ourselves uprooted from our historical mythological moorings. Furthermore, we can trace the impact of technology on family life to a number of important factors which influence individual psychological development as well. Robert Bly in his book about men (Iron John) states that one of the greatest casualties of the industrial revolution has been the family because father, and now mother, both work outside the home. Discussing all the ramifications of these influences would fill volumes and in fact have. The point I am attempting to make without being guilty of too many gross over simplification is that we live in a very complicated world. A world shaped by machines, a world in which most people don't know their neighbors and in which there isusually only one parent in a family. Most people live in cities and work in anonymous, large, impersonal, corporations.

The world I grew up in, small town America, in which neighbors knew each other, mothers were homemakers, and communal life revolved around church and school sports is largely a thing of the past. In most large cities there are several world religions represented by temples, mosques, synagogues, and churches. This kind of cultural and religious pluralism has resulted in many Gods being worshipped with equal fervor or indifference. For example, there was a discussion on television the other night which I found illuminating. Religious leaders from the Jewish, Protestant, and Muslim faiths were discussing the problems of hate crimes and prejudice. What I found so fascinating was that each had the religious conviction that theirs was the "true" God and their religion was "the path to righteousness." These belief systems now co—exist in the same neighborhoods. Each has his own "higher power".

So our predicament seems to me to be that many of the psychological problems we face today are a result of tremendous sociological and cultural forces unleashed by the industrial revolution and the impact of science on our ideology and family life. Though our basic human needs have largely remained the same, the world in which we exist is far different today than it was even in the 1950's.

Since, in my view, a fundamental psychological need is for meaning, significance and purpose, these profound cultural changes have left us in a crisis of faith. As Joseph Campbell commented, we have a demythologized world in which ritual, symbol, ceremony and myth have lost their power, resulting in many of our social problems today: violence, crime, divorce, suicide, the epidemic of substance abuse, and mental illness.

In his view, the function of mythology is to give people rules by which they can harmonize their lives with each other as well as makes sense of the universe and our place in it. When mythology loses its power, we are left with no rules, no models, and no explanations. Or probably more acccurately, rules that no longer fit our circumstances. The only explanations left are scientific. We are left with the need for a new paradigm. We need new mythologies which serve to bind us together, provide a window on the transcendent, inspire awe for the universe and provide individual guidelines for finding joy in life. Each of us needs an ideology which will bring us into accord with ourselves. But what does this digression have to do with recovery?

It seems as if we have come full circle. In the beginning of this work I stated that recovery and healing depend on our definition of the problem. Recovery from what? Healing from what? The answer to the questions depend on some sort of view

314

of the good life and presuppose an image of man and life based on a particular world view. In other words, it is crucial to our idea of recovery to understand what we think is wrong with us.

Whether we are atheists, Protestants, Catholics, Jews, Buddhists or Muslims, each of us has some sort of view about life which makes it meaningful and some views about how we should behave toward each other. I began this chapter with a quote from Campbell which suggested in choosing our God, we choose our view of the universe. I like this because it suggests to me that all of us end up using different language and metaphors to express our view of the universe. Paul Tillich, a theologian, called it our "ultimate concern".

What I am suggesting simply put, is that life is a spiritual journey and that there are principles which if discovered may lead to "enlightenment", the Kingdom of Heaven, Nirvana, Salvation, or whatever else you might prefer to call it. Some call it God, some, a higher power, but each of us has a metaphysic — a reason to be — which gives life a sense of the sacred. We must individually forge a reason to live out of the daily stuff of our lives. This is the fundamental realtionship between spirituality and recovery. In a sense, Recovery is a search for and an attempt to actualize the sacred in every day life.

When this ideology or reason to be loses its power, we face a profound spiritual crisis. This crisis creates a spiritual wasteland in which nothing makes sense. Samuel Beckett characterized our dilemma well in his play "Waiting

315

for Godot". We are just sitting around waiting. Sartre , in his play, "NO EXIT" depicted our existence as hell from which there is no release.

For those who find themselves in the depths of despair, this predicament in which we find no meaning, joy, or hope; God does indeed appear dead. This experience is the dark night of the soul, the valley of the shadow. We wander about alienated, full of self—loathing, and disgust. This condition is meaningfully depicted in the movie "The Fisher King". Jeff Bridges portrays the plight of a successful radio personality who has fallen from grace. He is depressed, life is meaningless, and he finds no joy in existence. He drowns his disgust with himself in alcohol. He goes to end it all and is paradoxically, rescued by Robin Williams who is portraying a psychotic homeless person. Each is redeemed as they learn to care for each other, and in that encouinter finds courage to face their own wounds. This, in my view, powerfully portrays our modern predicament and suggests some possible ways of looking at new myths. Perhaps since the Fisher King is based on the King Arthur legend of the Quest for the Holy Grail, it is really a new way of interpreting old myths and spiritual truths.

I have described the recovery process in the preceding chapters as a spiritual journey and have detailed many areas in which healing may take place. I have suggested practical, specific targets and ways of changing thinking, feeling and behaving. The problem which intrigues me is the relationship of the spiritual to the psychological and the ordinary commerce of our daily lives. It is this larger framework that undergirds the recovery process.

Is the life of faith and spirit still a relevant question for our day? If recovery is in some way related to spiritual forces, how are they related? If addiction is a spiritual problem, why even bother with all of this psychology business?

My approach is an attempt to integrate all of these questions by suggesting some ways in which the spiritual, the psychological and the daily are related and, in my view necessarily inter—related.

Soren Kierkegaard, a Danish philosopher, wrote an essay on the biblical story of Abraham, the Father of Judaism. In this story, Abraham hears the voice of God telling him to go up the mountain and build an altar, place his son on the altar and offer him as a sacrifice.

When I was a boy in Sunday School this story was told to me many times to illustrate how loyal and faithful Abraham was to obey God and how God rewards the obedient. I am sure at some level this is all there, but what Kierkegaard does for me is to focus on what Abraham might have gone through psychologically in this process.

Let's look at Abraham's dilemma as a parable about Faith that may illuminate our predicament. Just imagine, for a moment, that this happened to you. Think about it, you hear a voice telling you to go build an altar and kill your son. Sounds like Charles Manson, or any other psychotic child abuser we have read about. Or perhaps you have heard a voice telling you to kill yourself or go drink. Is this the voice

317

of God or madness? Who can tell us for sure? Is there anyone we can talk to about this? We are left alone in our situation.

How do we know it is the voice of God or perhaps just an auditory hallucination? This is the first problem confronting all of us. How are we to know, believe, and act on our inner impulses? Are they ones which are reliable? Most of us have had problems trusting our judgement, impulses and decisions in the past or we wouldn't be in a recovery program. Is it madness or is it Spirit calling us to set aside in our life a sacred place? This is a lonely place to be, few of us have the sky open up and experience a divine revelation. What happens if we ignore our inner urges and fail to find a sacredness in life? We appear to be in a dilemma for which there is no rational, certain, way of knowing what to do. This is just like life isn't it? Confusing, lonely, no place to hide, full of big decisions with awesome consequences. This requires *COURAGE,* which in my view, is a fundamental element required for authentic spirituality.

A second question which necessarily surfaces is Abraham's relationship with his son. Would any caring father kill his son as an act of obedience to God? Would a loving God ask that of us? Yet, again, in our daily lives we are faced with all the ways we hurt, abuse and neglect those we love. In the story we must confront the problem of how best to love those around us. What is the test of love? Is not the biggest problem in the world today the failure of each of us to love; ourselves, family, neighbor and earth itself? Do we not in many small ways betray the trust of others as well as sacrifice ourselves on the altar of addiction? In the Old Testament it is called Idolatry. Whatever we love we end up serving and becoming like.

So, then, in this relationship we are confronted with the second fundamental principle which integrates spirit, psyche, and the reality of life. *CARING* or love. What is a world without love? What happens when love fails and is replaced by hate? This is the most profound problem confronting us today: dealing with all of the destruction we have caused to ourselves, and those we care about. The irony is that most of us don't have the excuse of blaming it on God telling us to do it. We sacrificed ourselves and those we love, there is no one to blame. This illustrates a very fundamental concept: that which we love, that with which we identify, we become. In this sense, any addiction is a form of idolatry. As Paul Tillic so eloquently points out, we serve what ever is our ultimate concern. And conversely, love unifies, heals, sustains, and enlivens our very being. The failure of love and loving the wrong things destroys. Idolatry leads to spiritual impoverismnent.

A third foundational spiritual principle is a precondition of love. In order to love there must be a context, there must be people. We do not love in a vacuum. Hence, in our story we find Abraham performing his role as the patriarch of a tribe, a *COMMUNITY*. As I have indicated repeatedly, we become, we develop, we have our very identity tied to a community of people. It is the community which is held

319

together by common myths, values and ideals, that give birth to the individual. Again, it is the quality of community which determines the quality of life for its members.

I believe the problems we see today can be attributed to the failure of community. If there is community, for example, you do not throw rocks and burn down your neighbors' business. You do not drive by and fire an automatic pistol into your neighbors' living room if there is a community bound together by caring. Martin Buber, also another philosopher talks about the principle of I—thou relationships. In his view, it is in seeing the other person as a subject, that we manifest our humanity and the way that God is made present in human reality (Incarnation). When we relate to each other as objects (I—it) then we exploit, manipulate and violate the other because they are there for our narcissistic gratification. They exist only for what we can get out of them. Or in the case of violence, they are an object to be plundered or eliminated. When there is the divine spark in the other which we meet, recognize, and celebrate we establish the very foundation of being human and thereby unleash the healing and sustaining conditions for society to flourish. In our meeting we create the sacred in our very midst. As Scott Peck has put it, "It is only through Community that the world will be saved."

Abraham knew who he was, he knew what his role was, his son trusted him, and they existed in a community united by a historical tradition going back thousands of years. His behavior was rooted in ideas and a faith which affirmed him. His envelope was the community. In it he lived, moved and fulfilled his very individuality. In this reality, we find the dynamic tension which has the power to create the Kingdom of Heaven in our very midst. Without it, we have the very opposite.

Finally, another enduring principle of Spirit is **COMMITMENT.** None of the previous principles mean anything without commitment. We cannot love, we cannot experience community, unless we are committed.

Abraham, in his dilemma, could have spent years studying the problem of God. He could have formed committees to study the function of symbols and sacrifice in the community, or he could have ignored the problem altogether and just gone about business as usual. Lack of commitment is the source of emptiness and boredom which is the root of our spiritual malaise. Not only do we not find meaning in life, we find it tedious and burdensome when we are not engaged. We seem to be of the nature that we need significance, meaning, and purpose in order to find life worthwhile. Commitment becomes the vehicle for discovering the essence of life. In commitment we open ourselves up to the possibility of the moment. We allow ourselves to be deepened and stretched when we commit ourselves to a cause larger than ourselves. Abraham put his soul on the line when he decided to act, he risked it all. Without the risk of commitment we cannot experience the powerful richness of intimate relationships, the joy of raising and nurturing children and the deep satisfaction of belonging to a community of fellow believers. This act of engagement grounds us firmly in the sacredness of the moment.

Addiction and other human afflictions seem to be an outgrowth of our spiritual difficulties in this peculiar age. As we try to live our ordinary lives, we often feel lost, lonely, isolated, alienated and estranged from any genuine relationships. We belong to nothing, do nothing, feel nothing, believe nothing and care about nothing. As a defense, we use chemicals to dull the pain or create a false sense of being alive. In pursuit of greater and greater sensations, we burn out and collapse. This is not a fertile ground for psychological, social or spiritual well—being. It is in fact the very ground in which perversions and fetishized existnece flourishes. What is needed for healing? *COURAGE, CARING, COMMUNITY and COMMITMENT. In a word, Faith.* A faith which becomes the centering act of our personalities and grounds us in a life pursuit of spiritual enrichment.

In this work I have sought to develop a perspective which would lead to both a way of looking at addiction and other psychological problems, as well as a way of approaching them.

I have suggested that one way to view the problem is to see life differently. That perhaps what is needed is a way of looking at things which will provide a foundation for living that will lead to a sense of meaning, purpose and significance: a meaning framework or reason to be.

I would like to take these few remaining pages to enlarge on this idea and share some ideas which have been helpful to me in my own struggle. I have borrowed from Joseph Campbell heavily for his ideas on the "Hero's Journey". The concept of the Hero's Journey is based on a view of life which places supreme value on life as a spiritual journey. This transforms everything when this perspective is used to look at life. In contrast to life as a spiritual process there is the alternative of materialism which would view the purpose of life as deriving the greatest pleasure from the acquisition of things. The credo of this perspective is "He who dies with the most toys wins." The gold card, a house in suburbia, great job, and bank account become the definers of our worth and identity.

The purpose of life in the Hero's Journey is transformation of the self through an inward journey which leads to enlightenment and sense of aliveness.

The Hero's Journey then is inward, to the very center of the self. The goal of this journey is transformation of consciousness, behavior and life as lived by the traveler. When viewed this way, everything in life is an instrument of enlightenment. Every problem is an opportunity to learn about ourselves.

The Hero's Journey begins with the call to adventure. Who is the Hero? The hero is anyone who is a seeker after the life of the spirit. As Campbell phrases it "the hero is symbolic of that divine creative and redemptive image which is hidden within us all only waiting to be known and rendered into life."

The hero deed that needs to be brought about today, he says, is to render the world spiritually significant. That is, to make it possible for men and women to come to full maturity through the conditions of contemporary life. It is confrontation with the hero task which becomes the heroics of every day life.

Campbell concludes his book, *The Hero With A Thousand Faces* with the following observation:

It is not society that is to guide and save the creative hero, but precisely the reverse. And so everyone of us shares the supreme ideal — carries the cross of the redeemer — not in the bright moments of his tribes great victories, but in the silence of his personal despair. (p391)

The Hero's Journey requires courage because it means facing our own despair. In fact, the journey begins on the threshold of despair. It is precisely at the moment you sense that your life is not working and you feel the terrifying vulnerability of being out of control and the spirit deadening futility of hopelessness that you are being called to the great adventure. None of us likes to know this, but the journey always begins with the wound. Or as some call it, hitting bottomm.

You can turn back and redouble your efforts at what you were doing that got you here or you can heed the call; cross the threshold and commit yourself to the inward journey that will lead to transformation. The wound, the wasteland of your disillusionment, is the starting place. You must care enough for yourself to commit to this journey. *CARING, COURAGE, COMMUNITY, and COMMITMENT* lead to healing. As we address our wounds, we are led to self—discovery which leads to compassion and takes away the blindness that has been the cause of our self destructiveness. "Know yourself" becomes the new credo. When you commit to the journey you will stand in the community of spiritual pilgrims from all the great hero systems and see them as the masks of God. This leads to a healing accord with ourselves, others and life itself. This is the sacredness of the journey which transforms the struggles of daily life.

> *The mystery of life is*
> *not a problem to be*
> *solved but a reality*
> *to be experienced.*
> *And that mystery,*
> *that deep, deep, ever*
> *so deep thing which*
> *is before all worlds*
> *is you, the unrecognized*
> *SELF.*
> *Alan Watts*

> *What shall it profit a*
> *man if he gains the*
> *whole world but*
> *loses his soul?*
> *The Bible*

What do you say will lead you out of your own wilderness?

CHAPTER 11

THE HERO'S JOURNEY

EXERCISE 1

1. Assume a miracle has happened and you have achieved your recovery goals.

   How is your life different?

2. What of yourself and your present life is the same and you would like to see continue?

CHAPTER 11

THE HEROE'S JOURNEY

EXERCISE 2

1. Imagine that you have grown to be a healthy and wise older person.

   A. What do you think this wise person would suggest to you to continue your recovery?

   B. What would this person see in you that would be a solid foundation for recovery?

   C. What would this person say to give you hope and comfort?

CHAPTER 11

THE HEROE'S JOURNEY

EXERCISE 3

1. What differences will your recovery make in how you feel about you?

2. What differences will your recovery make in the way your significant others see you?

3. What differences will your recovery make to future generations of your family?

CHAPTER 11

THE HEROE'S JOURNEY

EXERCISE 4

1. Identify beliefs, rituals, and ceremonies which gave you peace, hope, and comfort as a child?

2. What are the things which give you meaning, purpose, significance and make your life worthwhile now?

CHAPTER 11

THE HEROE'S JOURNEY

EXERCISE 5

1. Imagine you are going on a long journey. Who would you want to go with you and what would you take as part of your survival kit?

2. Of all the things in your life, what are the ones you can least do without?

CHAPTER 11

THE HEROE'S JOURNEY

EXERCISE 6

1. Define for yourself what it would take for you to feel fulfilled as a person?

   What obstacles are in the way?

   What do you feel are your most important life purposes?

2. Visualize for ten minutes a day what your life would look like if you were to realize your unique identity quest.

CHAPTER 11

THE HEROE'S JOURNEY

EXERCISE 7

1. Develop a reading list that emphasizes spiritual matters. If you have a personal religion spend time each day reading a passage or chapter and meditate on it periodically throughout the day.

2. If you do not have a personal faith read something from each of the world's religions or any thing else which inspires you.

3. Spend 10—15 minutes a day meditating on a theme such as peace, joy, hope, love, etc. Do it until you experience it.

4. Make a list of spiritual affirmations and carry them with you. Refer to them often during the day.

CHAPTER 11

THE HEROE'S JOURNEY

EXERCISE 8

Connecting With Your Spiritual Power

1. Find and attend a spiritual community; become a part of it's life.

2. Using the techniques we have practiced, visualize a special place you can go to and commune with your higher power.

   a. Let yourself be there. Experience the peace, comfort, and awe of the connection.

   b. Talk to your spiritual guide. What do you need to know? What do you need to do? Practice this whenever you need to.

   c. Listen to the tape "Affirmations".

CHAPTER 11

THE HEROE'S JOURNEY

EXERCISE 9

1. Learning to care can be very difficult if you have been hurt, disappointed or had a history where caring was associated with violence, abuse or trauma. Learning to care can begin with simple, single acts in which you find something outside yourself to care for. Caring is the act of becoming re—attached and involved with life again.

   For example: Two years ago I was lying in bed, depressed and hating my life and I looked at my bedroom ceiling and noticed how I hated the wallpaper. I decided to change it. First the ceiling, then the walls, then the trim, etc.

   I ended up with a two year project in which I completely restored the house. In the process, I restored myself. The project culminated in building a deck behind the house. My son and I spent 3 months designing and building the deck. The three months together also restored our relationship.

   A. Pick a project, anything that you perhaps have always wanted to do. Spend time caring for it. Involve yourself, give yourself, spend time and effort on it. I have a client whose recovery from cocaine addiction began with getting a dog that she had to take care of.

   B. Volunteer your services to an agency that needs people. Giving of yourself is another act of caring and getting involved in something larger than yourself.

   C. Find a cause: save the world by doing something in your little corner. Devote time, energy, and yourself. In caring, you will save yourself.

CHAPTER 11

THE HEROE'S JOURNEY

FURTHER READING

Campbell, Joseph. The Hero With A Thousand Faces. New Jersey: Princeton University. 1973.

Campbell, Joseph. Myths to Live By. New York: Bantam Books. 1982.

Castanada, Carlos. Journey to Ixtlan. New York: Simon and Shuster. 1972.

Hahn, T. H. The Miracle of Mindfulness: A Manual on Meditation. Boston: Beacon Pess. 1976.

Keen, Sam. To A Dancing God. New York: Harper and Row. 1990.

Matthiessen, Peter. The Snow Leopard. Boston: Shambbala. 1979.

Moore, Thomas. The Care of The Soul. New York: Harper Collins. 1992.

Peck, M. Scott. The Different Drum. New York: Simon & Schuster. 1987.

Tillich, Paul. The Dynamics of Faith. New York: Harper and Row, 1957.

Watts, Alan. The Spirit of Zen. New York: Grove Press. 1958.

Zukav, Gary. The Seat of The Soul New York: Fireside Books. 1990.

NOTES

The Hero's Journey: A Course on self-esteem

by Gary W. Reece, Ph.D.

Dr. Reece, combines his unique skills in this book of meditations which are designed to increase awareness, inner healing and transformation of wounded self-esteem. The book is designed to teach each individual how to discover their inner sense of worth and significance by using guided imagery, journaling, intensive self-exploration, relaxation, meditation, and visualization He utilizes a three stage experiential approach:

1. RECOGNIZE: In this stage the attitudes, thoughts, ideas and self-talk (cognitive domain) are explored along with strategies for changing long held and deeply ingrained habits of thought, self-talk, attitudes and expextations.

2. VISUALIZE: Techniques for Guided Imagery, relaxation, meditation, and visualization are used to intensify the transformation process. The person is encouraged to take the inner journey of self-exploration to reconnect with the inner resources of power and vitality which empower the journey to self-esteem.

3. ACTUALIZE: Strategies for integrating feelings, imagery, awareness, thoughts, and behaviors for consciously transforming self-esteem are taught so that each individual may become the architect and creator of their emerging self.

To continue your recovery journey order this outstanding and inspirational book on self-esteem by turning the page.

THE STEPCARE INSTITUTE

Programs and seminars of interest to individuals, institutions and professionals are offered on a regular basis by the Institute. Training and consultation services are offered in the area of trauma, bereavement, addiction, crisis intervention, stress management and recovery.

If you or your organization would like to discuss programs, consultation, or training Dr. Reece is available to help you design and implement a program to fit your needs.

Available Educational Materials

Trauma Loss & Bereavement   **$20.00**
The Hero's Journey: A course on Self-Esteem   **$35.00**
Audio Tape Series--Relaxation, Inner Journey, Self-Esteem $20.00

Significant discounts on bulk purchases for institutions are available, please inquire. You may order by contacting

The STEPCARE INSTITUTE
451 W. Sierra Madre Blvd. Ste. N
Sierra Madre, CA 91024

For more information call **626 355 2407** or **e mail** greecephd@earthlink.net
web page **www.stepcare.org**

If you would like to order educational materials please fill out the form below

Name_____

Title _____ Quantity _____ Price _____
Title _____ Quantity _____ Price _____
Address_____
City _____ State _____ ZIP_____
Phone _____ Fax _____ Total _____
Add   *$5.00 for shipping and handling*